Moonlight

This book helps readers understand *Moonlight*'s profound political and social importance, the innovative technical choices adopted by director Barry Jenkins and the film's adoption and disruption of traditional coming-of-age themes through the specific prism of Chiron's childhood and youth. *Moonlight* (2016) is an intensely moving and poetically rendered coming-of-age story about a young gay Black boy, Chiron. Highly praised by both critics and audiences internationally, it garnered a surprise Best Picture win at the 2017 Academy Awards, enshrining its significance within a global cinematic canon. This book provides an account of how *Moonlight* can be situated in relation to African American youth films, contemporary queer cinema and its appeal to the youth market and representations of non-normative childhood and adolescence. It analyses the reception of *Moonlight* in terms of its form and profound emotional impact on spectators offering new visions of African American boyhoods while also contributing an extended exploration of the social and political context of the film in relation to Obama, Trump and diversity in filmmaking.

Highlighting to students and scholars the powerful emotional pull of *Moonlight* and why it is a highly significant film, this book is ideal for those interested in critical race studies, queer theory, youth cinema, African American cinema and LGBTQ cinema.

Maria Flood is Lecturer in World Cinema at Liverpool University. She is the author of *France, Algeria and the Moving Image* (2017) and has published on Francophone cinemas of the Maghreb, world cinema and political violence and terrorism and ethics in documentary film.

Cinema and Youth Cultures

Cinema and Youth Cultures engages with well-known youth films from American cinema as well the cinemas of other countries. Using a variety of methodological and critical approaches, the series volumes provide informed accounts of how young people have been represented in film while also exploring the ways in which young people engage with films made for and about them. In doing this, the Cinema and Youth Cultures series contributes to important and long-standing debates about youth cultures, how these are mobilized and articulated in influential film texts and the impact that these texts have had on popular culture at large.

Series Editors: Siân Lincoln and Yannis Tzioumakis

Gidget
Origins of a Teen Girl Transmedia Franchise
Pamela Robertson Wojcik

The Beatles and Film
From Youth Culture to Counterculture
Stephen Glynn

Clerks
'Over the Counter' Culture and Youth Cinema
Peter Templeton

Moonlight
Screening Black Queer Youth
Maria Flood

For more information about this series, please visit: https://www.routledge.com/Cinema-and-Youth-Cultures/book-series/CYC

Moonlight

Screening Black Queer Youth

Maria Flood

Routledge
Taylor & Francis Group

LONDON AND NEW YORK

First published 2022
by Routledge
2 Park Square, Milton Park, Abingdon, Oxon OX14 4RN

and by Routledge
605 Third Avenue, New York, NY 10158

Routledge is an imprint of the Taylor & Francis Group, an informa business

British Library Cataloguing-in-Publication Data
A catalogue record for this book is available from the British Library

Library of Congress Cataloging-in-Publication Data
Names: Flood, Maria, author.
Title: Moonlight: screening black queer youth/Maria Flood.
Description: Abingdon, Oxon; New York: Routledge, 2022. |
Series: Cinema youth cultures | Includes bibliographical references
and index.
Identifiers: LCCN 2021029543 (print) | LCCN 2021029544 (ebook) |
ISBN 9780367151393 (hardback) | ISBN 9781032152066 (paperback) |
ISBN 9780429055294 (ebook)
Subjects: LCSH: Moonlight (Motion picture: 2016) | African Americans in
motion pictures. | Homosexuality in motion pictures. | Sexual minorities in
motion pictures.
Classification: LCC PN1997.2.M6456 F56 2022 (print) |
LCC PN1997.2.M6456 (ebook) | DDC 791.43/72–dc23
LC record available at https://lccn.loc.gov/2021029543
LC ebook record available at https://lccn.loc.gov/2021029544

ISBN: 978-0-367-15139-3 (hbk)
ISBN: 978-1-032-15206-6 (pbk)
ISBN: 978-0-429-05529-4 (ebk)

DOI: 10.4324/9780429055294

Typeset in Times New Roman
by Deanta Global Publishing Services, Chennai, India

Contents

Figures

Series Editors' Introduction

Despite the high visibility of youth films in the global media marketplace, especially since the 1980s when Conglomerate Hollywood realized that such films were not only strong box office performers but also the starting point for ancillary sales in other media markets as well as for franchise building, academic studies that focused specifically on such films were slow to materialize. Arguably, the most important factor behind academia's reluctance to engage with youth films was a (then) widespread perception within the film and media studies communities that such films held little cultural value and significance and, therefore, were not worthy of serious scholarly research and examination. Just like the young subjects they represented, whose interests and cultural practices have been routinely deemed transitional and transitory, so too were the films that represented them perceived as fleeting and easily digestible, destined to be forgotten quickly, as soon as the next youth film arrived in cinema screens a week later.

Under these circumstances, and despite a small number of pioneering studies in the 1980s and early 1990s, the field of 'youth film studies' did not really start blossoming and attracting significant scholarly attention until the 2000s and in combination with similar developments in cognate areas, such as 'girl studies'. However, because of the paucity of material in the previous decades, the majority of these new studies in the 2000s focused primarily on charting the field and, therefore, steered clear of long, in-depth examinations of youth films or were exemplified by edited collections that chose particular films to highlight certain issues to the detriment of others. In other words, despite providing often wonderfully rich accounts of youth cultures captured by key films, these studies could not possibly have dedicated sufficient space to engage with more than just a few key aspects of youth films.

In more recent (post-2010) years, a number of academic studies started delimiting their focus and, therefore, providing more space for in-depth examinations of key types of youth films, such as slasher films and biker films or examining youth films in particular historical periods. From that point on, it was a matter of time for the first publications that focused exclusively on key youth films from a number of perspectives to appear (*Mamma Mia! The Movie*, *Twilight* and *Dirty Dancing* are among the first films to receive this treatment). Conceived primarily as edited collections, these studies provided a multifaceted analysis of these films, focusing on such issues as the politics of representing youth, the stylistic and narrative choices that characterize these films and the extent to which they are representative of a youth cinema, the ways these films address their audiences, the ways youth audiences engage with these films, the films' industrial location and other relevant issues.

It is within this increasingly maturing and expanding academic environment that the Cinema and Youth Cultures volumes arrive, aiming to consolidate existing knowledge, provide new perspectives, apply innovative methodological approaches and offer sustained and in-depth analyses of key films and, therefore, become the 'go to' resource for students and scholars interested in theoretically informed, authoritative accounts of youth cultures in film. As editors, we have tried to be as inclusive as possible in our selection of key examples of youth films by commissioning volumes on films that span the history of cinema, including the silent film era, that portray contemporary youth cultures as well as ones associated with particular historical periods, represent examples of mainstream and independent cinema. originate in American cinema and the cinemas of other nations, have attracted significant critical attention and commercial success during their initial release and were 'rediscovered' after an unpromising initial critical reception. Together, these volumes are going to advance youth film studies while also being able to offer extremely detailed examinations of films that are now considered significant contributions to cinema and our cultural life more broadly.

We hope readers will enjoy the series.
Siân Lincoln & Yannis Tzioumakis
Cinema & Youth Cultures Series Editors

Acknowledgements

I want to first express my sincere gratitude to the editors of the series, Yannis Tzioumakis and Siân Lincoln, who have been incredibly enthusiastic, helpful and generous throughout. My thanks also go to the anonymous readers who provided such useful feedback at the proposal stage. I would also like to express appreciation for my colleagues and students at Keele University who have assisted in various ways in the completion of this project, as well as my contemporaries at the Society for the Humanities at Cornell University. Particular thanks go to the following friends and colleagues: Ricardo Wilson, Jenny Chamarette, Eva Giraud, Mariangela Palladino, Susan Bruce, Becky Bowler and Jessica Eley. My love and thanks, as always, go to my sisters, nieces and parents for being supportive and kind, even as time and space separated us for months and years during the pandemic. Special praise goes to my Dad, who read most of the draft chapters and provided detailed handwritten feedback that he then posted to the UK. My gratitude and love also go to my partner Alan who put up with me in the long dark days of January 2021 when I became a ghost in a dressing gown that did nothing but eat, sleep, and write. I should also give a little mention to Tess, who has been a faithful and fluffy friend through it all.

Moonlight is a film about the endurance and importance of friendship and love, and so I want to dedicate this book to friends, those who are here and those who have gone.

To Damien Mooney, la fabuleuse, without whom this book wouldn't exist.

To Zoë Foley, who has known me at all the stages of my life – go on the Woogies!

Finally, to Sinéad Flattery and James Harrington: Sinéad, for all the mischief of our childhood (that bite), and James, for the naughtiness of our 20s (we'll always have Paris).

I miss you both.

Introduction

Moonlight, directed by Barry Jenkins, is an intensely moving and poetically rendered coming-of-age story about a young gay Black boy, Chiron. Set in the Miami neighbourhood of Liberty City, the film charts three stages of Chiron's life from the 1980s to the 1990s. *Moonlight* is based on the unproduced play *In Moonlight Black Boys Look Blue* by Tarell Alvin McCraney, a McArthur Grant-winning playwright. Made with a budget of an estimated $1.5 million, the film went on to achieve a worldwide gross of $65 million (Brueggenmann 2017; Anon. 2021a). As of April 2021, the film has won 222 awards, including the Oscar for Best Picture and the Best Adapted Screenplay for Jenkins and McCraney (Anon. 2021b). *Moonlight* garnered almost universal critical praise, in both established media outlets, such as the *Guardian*, the *New York Times*, and the *Washington Post*, as well as in online forums, including Black and queer websites and social media. As Soraya Nadia McDonald notes, 'for once, it's safe to believe the hype: *Moonlight* is just as extraordinary as the continuous stream of glowing praise it's been receiving would have you believe' (2016). Since *Moonlight*, Jenkins has directed a critically acclaimed film adaptation of James Baldwin's *If Beale Street Could Talk* (2018) and an Amazon mini-series adaptation of Colson Whitehead's groundbreaking novel *The Underground Railroad* (2021).

The great tenderness with which Jenkins treats his subject matter contributed to the film's astonishing success. The story is told in three distinct, individually titled segments with a different actor playing Chiron in each part of the triptych: 'I - Little' (Alex R. Hibbert), 'II - Chiron' (Ashton Sanders) and 'III - Black' (Trevante Rhodes). We witness the child 'Little' experience bullying from classmates and harsh treatment from his mother Paula (Naomi Harris) and his tentative rescue and respite from this world through the care of Juan (Mahershala Ali) and his girlfriend Teresa (Janelle Monáe). In the second section, the adolescent Chiron, a shy and awkward teenager, struggles with his mother's growing drug addiction and the increasing torments of the bullies at school. A caring, romantic and sexual

DOI: 10.4324/9780429055294-101

encounter with his friend Kevin (Jharrel Jerome) on the beach is followed by deep betrayal. The final section introduces the adult Chiron, now calling himself Black, a tough, heavy-set and muscular figure, whose hard public persona is at odds with the private vulnerability he displays in moments of quietude.

Moonlight is at once highly personal and decisively political. As A.O. Scott writes in the *New York Times*, '*Moonlight* is both a disarmingly, at times almost unbearably personal film and an urgent social document' (2016a). Its importance goes far beyond its Oscar wins: as a queer Black love story, it speaks to the themes and styles of both queer and African American cinemas while also evoking the techniques and influences of European and Hollywood cinema. The film touches on a number of significant socio-political themes: the ghettoization of African American neighbourhoods, racist government policy and the devastating 'war on drugs', drug addiction, queer youth, homophobia, the prison industrial complex and masculinity. It also offers a moving meditation on childhood vulnerability, youthful identity formation and the transformative possibilities of empathy and love. As Menaka Kannan, Rhys Hall and Matthew Hughey summarize, *Moonlight* asks 'who am I going to be, and to what extent will I decide for myself, or will I let society decide for me the course of my life?' (2017: 288).

This book is divided into five chapters, each of which tackles a key issue or context in relation to *Moonlight*. The first chapter offers an overview of the socio-political contexts of the film's creation: released in the autumn of 2016, *Moonlight* was poised between the end of the Obama era and the election of Trump. This was also an era of change and controversy in Hollywood, when debates about diversity, both in front and behind the camera, reached a zenith in the Academy, notably through the campaign '#OscarsSoWhite'. The second chapter examines *Moonlight*'s treatment of Black masculinity on screen, one of the major themes of the film. I examine it in relation to histories of stereotyping in Hollywood and two Black film movements that significantly engaged with ideas of youth and Black masculinity, Blaxploitation and New Black Realism. In the third chapter, I consider *Moonlight*'s status as a queer film, tracking a concise history of Black queer film and arguing that Chiron's sexuality must be understood alongside his race and his socio-economic background. The fourth chapter considers the form and techniques of *Moonlight* and its beauty, and in so doing, it looks at narrative structure, cinematography, space, colour and music symbolism in the film. Finally, Chapter 5 considers some of the debates around empathy, universality and specificity that were generated in the popular reception of the film, connecting these discussions to the film's innovative presentation of Black boyhood and youth.

In this introduction, I also want to address my own motivations in writing this book. I grew up a white girl from a small town in rural Ireland. As a teenager, I will not say I simply got involved with the wrong crowd – I was very much in and of the wrong crowd. Eventually, I was given a second and third chance to change my ways. There was some violence in this experience but also a lot of compassion and love. In the end, I came out of it feeling that a gap had been opened between the child that I was, the teenager I became and the adult who looked back on it all. I do not know if I will ever see a film like *Moonlight* again, one that captures with such intensity that sense of a life broken into three distinct fragments that, perhaps, over time, fuse disjointedly together.

Yet, while I am deeply moved by the film on a personal basis, I am also acutely aware that the prism of the coming-of-age narrative is only one of the many ways one can understand, approach and feel for *Moonlight*. In Chapter 5, I consider the relationship between the film's wide appeal and its specific emotional, intellectual and political investments in queer and Black communities and artistic traditions. Throughout the book, I have relied on the work of critical race theorists, queer theorists and Black and queer critics to guide the readings of the film that I present here, some of which are my own, many of which are the interpretations of others. Many readers will be familiar with this work, but for those who are not, I hope that this book directs them toward these sources. I am grateful to friends and colleagues at the Society for the Humanities at Cornell University for initially guiding me toward this work.

A quote from bell hooks illuminates a form of reading and viewing practice I have tried to adopt throughout. Speaking about a portrait of Billy Holiday by photographer Moneta Sleet in which Holiday appears melancholy and pensive in contrast to the many bright publicity images of the star, hooks writes: 'when I face this image, this black look, something inside me is shattered. I have to pick up the bits and pieces of myself and start all over again – transformed by the image' (2014: 7). Reading this quote, I understand that I do not feel the same as hooks in the face of this image, and I cannot claim alignment or identification with the specificities of hooks's experience nor that of Chiron; however, her words invite me to look again and to marvel at the emotional power of images – a power that is shaped by and depends on the life of the looker and the context of looking. These encounters between visual cultures, their makers, viewers and interpreters are the productive spaces that make art compelling, vibrant, urgent and necessary. But they are also singular and depend on complex histories and politics that not every artist, viewer or writer shares, and these differences must be acknowledged in our acts of interpretation. Sara Ahmed also references an approach to emotion and interpretation that acknowledges difference when describing how we might engage with the painful experiences of others. She notes that, while we may feel we know pain, acknowledging the pain of another person 'involves being open to being affected by that which one cannot know or feel' (2014: 30). Ultimately, she argues that a collective politics might be based not on declarations of similarity but 'on learning that we live with and beside each other, and yet we are not as one' (p. 39).

I first heard of *Moonlight* on the radio as I was driving home in my car from the university campus. What stood out immediately from the presenter's description of the film was its three-part structure, which so clearly demarcated the three stages of Chiron's life. Later, having watched the film, I was moved to tears by this tracing of how the world moulds and shapes a young person, for, as the film's promotional slogan notes, 'this is the story of a lifetime'. Of course, the film does not quite chart a lifetime, and one hopes that, somewhere in the ether of imagination, Chiron and Kevin live on, perhaps near the South Florida ocean, drinking their wine, water, and green tea, with Kevin still teasing Chiron for his quietness. However, in plotting the transition from childhood to adulthood, *Moonlight* captures the ways this period of growth can feel like a lifespan for those who are experiencing it; so dense is the web of experiences that young people undergo. Certainly, *Moonlight* speaks to younger audiences, and I would not have embarked on this book project without the love and enthusiasm my students have expressed for the film in the four years that I have taught it at Keele University. The insights and reflections that they shared in class are part of the fabric of this book, and I am grateful to them.

1 'A film we've been waiting for'

The social and cultural contexts of *Moonlight*

Moonlight debuted in cinemas on 21 October 2016, just before Donald Trump's election as the 45th president of the United States. Telling the story of a Black boy growing up in an impoverished neighbourhood as he struggles with his sexuality, bullying and his mother's addiction, the film precisely captures the kinds of queer, Black and minority lives and voices that the rhetoric of the Trump campaign both excluded and targeted. *Moonlight* thus evokes the ambiguities of this particular political moment: the hopeful Obama years, the rising recognition of minority voices in media and film and the election of Trump, whose political manoeuvrings encapsulate for many the kinds of structural violence and inequalities that *Moonlight* so carefully gestures toward. Chapter 1 of this book examines the creative, social and political contexts surrounding the film's production and reception, within the context of the end of the Obama era, the election of Trump and '#OscarsSoWhite'.

The background of *Moonlight*: Jenkins and McCraney

Moonlight can be described as a film of firsts, and it beat the odds at the 89th Academy Awards ceremony in 2017 to win Best Picture against Damien Chazelle's *La La Land*. Indeed, *La La Land*, Hollywood's homage to Hollywood, was initially falsely announced as the winner by Warren Beatty and Faye Dunaway. In spite of this awkward and chaotic mix up, *Moonlight*'s triumphs at the ceremony were numerous. Joi McMillon received the first nomination for a Black woman for editing, Mahershala Ali won the first Oscar for a Muslim actor and the film was the first with an all-Black cast and LGBTQ themes to win Oscars for Best Picture and Best Adapted Screenplay. These pioneering achievements led critics to describe *Moonlight* in glowing terms: the *Los Angeles Times* called it 'a film we've been waiting for for a very long time' (Turan 2016), and Farihah Zaman described *Moonlight* as 'a necessary film for this moment in time' (2016:

DOI: 10.4324/9780429055294-1

42). The film has appeared on more than 51 critics' top ten lists for 2016, and on Metacritic, the film comes a close second to another coming-of-age drama, Richard Linklater's *Boyhood* (2014), for the 'Best Film of the 2010s' (Dietz 2019).

However, although many critics described it as a much needed and longed-for cinematic event, *Moonlight* very nearly did not get made. Jenkins was enrolled in Florida State University when he happened to see a poster for film school. Signing up for the programme, he dropped out after a year, feeling that he did not have enough cinematic knowledge to continue the degree at that time. Rather than watching classic Hollywood works, he immersed himself in foreign cinema, particularly French and Hong Kong auteur cinema. Returning to film school, Jenkins made his first documentary short, *My Josephine* (2003), about an Arab American laundry that cleaned American flags free of charge after 9/11. Following a few peripatetic years (he moved to Los Angeles, worked for Oprah Winfrey, relocated to San Francisco, had his heart broken, loaded boxes for Banana Republic), Jenkins returned to directing with the feature length *Medicine for Melancholy* (2008), a film that addresses the social and romantic connections between two African American hipsters. Following a one-night stand, the pair wander through the rapidly changing streets of San Francisco, uncovering spatial and racial histories and grappling with the personal ramifications of the woman's (absent) white boyfriend. The interweaving of the social and the stylistic are already evident: shot in a washed out, sepia-hued fade, the couple discuss the increasing gentrification of the city as they tentatively explore their burgeoning romantic bond.

Yet, it would take Jenkins another eight years to complete *Moonlight*, during which time he had started a number of other projects. The revelation came about when he reunited with Adele Romanski, a producer friend he had fallen out with, and was sent the unproduced script of McCraney's semi-autobiographical stage play *In Moonlight Black Boys Look Blue*. Jenkins was struck by how similar the two men's childhoods had been and how much of his own story was mirrored in McCraney's text: both men grew up in the impoverished Liberty City area of Miami in the 1980s, and both had mothers who struggled with drug addiction. Yet, when he described his idea for the film to friends and colleagues, many told him that making *Moonlight* would be 'career suicide' (Anderson-Moore 2018), particularly because of the use of unknown actors and the three-part structure of the film.

The story of *Moonlight* was deeply personal to both Jenkins and McCraney, yet Jenkins is careful to draw distinctions between his story and McCraney's: McCraney identifies as a gay man, Jenkins as straight. Moreover, in advice offered to young filmmakers in the 'No Film School' online community, Jenkins states that an aspiring director should make their films 'not biographical, but personal' (Anderson-Moore 2018). *Moonlight*, then, tells Jenkins's story at a slant – he shares Chiron's upbringing but not the main character's anguished relation to his sexuality. For McCraney, however, watching *Moonlight* felt 'too close'; he notes that in repeat viewings of the film, 'I actually ended up feeling that these are still looming questions in my life, questions about my own identity and my own self-worth that I'm still trying to figure out' (quoted in Lee 2016).

The political contexts of *Moonlight* 1: Barack Obama – the first Black president and the 'first gay president'

Andrew Pulver describes Jenkins's ascent from Liberty City to Oscar glory as 'a scramble up the foothills of the American dream' (2016). This 'scramble' becomes all the more pertinent given the political context in which *Moonlight* was released: at the end of the Obama years and as the Trump presidency loomed. The American Dream is an ideal of progress, the notion that one will be wealthier and more secure than one's parents and one's children will be better again. It is also a dream of triumph over adversity in which the individual overcomes nearly insurmountable odds, enduring suffering to achieve almost unimaginable success (see Hochschild 2016). This is Jenkins's story, that of a poor Black boy in America who grows up to make an artistically innovative, widely distributed, financially successful film that achieves an astonishing number of accolades.

Jenkins's path toward the American Dream also has parallels with the story of Barack Obama, who, on 4 November 2008, became the first African American to be elected president in the country's 232-year history. Indeed, given the long history of racial oppression of African Americans in the US, Obama's election was noteworthy in and of itself. But the 44th US president also carefully highlighted the challenges he faced, most notably growing up (like Jenkins and McCraney) in a single-parent household that faced intermittent financial difficulties:

> 'My father left my mother when I was two years old, and I was raised by a single mother who struggled at times to pay the bills and wasn't always able to give us things the other kids had. There were times when I missed having a father in my life'.
>
> (Obama 2009)

The enormous political and symbolic significance of having a Black American president cannot be underestimated: the 2008 election led to 'unprecedented diversity' in the electoral turnout (Anon. 2009), with up to 90% of African American voters selecting Obama as their candidate

(Sullivan and Johnson 2008: 51). Obama did place race on the agenda, noting the structural inequalities that held back Black advancement in the US, while also recognizing the role of class and income disparities (Obama 2013). Research also suggests that on a symbolic level, Obama's presidency did help reduce the 'black male = threat' stereotype, held consciously or unconsciously, with Jennifer Richeson and Meghan Bean arguing that 'consistent exposure' to Obama through the media reduced racial bias (2011: 100). Indeed, in relation to Obama's presidency, Kannan et al. suggest that a film like *Moonlight* 'could not have been made (or at least would be unlikely to receive critical praise), if not for the last eight years' (2017: 288). Thus, the cultural visibility of Obama allowed for a burgeoning of interest in creative works that were not exclusively or principally focused on white characters and contexts.

Obama was also hailed as 'the first gay president' by weekly magazine *Newsweek* on 21 May 2012, because of his declared support for gay marriage rights on *Good Morning America* four days earlier. Obama is not gay, and this designation belies a history of inconsistent support for LGBT rights in the US (Goldstein 2011). Before 2012, Obama declared his support for equal rights for LGBT people but not marriage equality. However, for many commentators, this declaration, albeit belated, was enormously significant. The announcement came months before the 2012 election and led journalists to describe the move as 'Obama's gay marriage backing gamble' (Kingstone 2012). Dylan Stableford recognizes that while 'the interview change[d] no laws [and] ha[d] no tangible effect', he nonetheless thought of 'all the gay kids out there who now know they have their president on their side' (2012). Obama's presidency also saw the legalization of gay marriage, when on 28 April 2015, in the case of *Obergefell v. Hodges*, the Supreme Court ruled 5-4 that the fundamental right to marry is guaranteed to same-sex couples across all 50 states.

As an embodiment of the American Dream of overcoming the odds and achieving material and social success through hard work and education, it is perhaps unsurprising that a number of Obama's speeches held onto the key tenets of the 'Dream', with its reliance on ideologies of individualism. In his election speech on 7 November 2008, he notes that his mother, 'raised my sister and me to believe that in America there are no barriers to success – no matter what color you are, no matter where you're from, no matter how much money you have' (Obama 2007). This is a belief that is borne out by his own life story, and one that led many white commentators on both the left and the right of the political spectrum to proclaim that America had become a 'post-racial' society.

The term 'post-racial' relates to a society in which racism and racial discrimination no longer exist, one in which 'Americans begin to make race-free judgments on who should lead them' (Schorr 2008). In 2008, National Public Radio political analyst Daniel Schorr posited that, while it may be too early to say that votes are colour blind, they might be 'color blurred' (Schorr 2008), and in 2009, conservative radio host Lou Dobbs called twenty-first-century America a 'post-partisan, post-racial' society (quoted in Dawson and Bobo 2009: 247). Bill Bennett, former education secretary under Reagan, stated '[Obama] never brings race into it. He never plays the race card' (quoted in Hughey 2011: 20). Even actor Will Smith argued that, with the election of Obama, 'African American excuses have been removed. There's no white man trying to keep you down, because if he were really trying to keep you down, he would have done everything he could to keep Obama down' (quoted in Mendick et al. 2018: 57). Such rhetoric feeds into the notion that racial inequality was a myth, and rather factors such as family dysfunction and dissolution in Black families (referenced by Obama in a 2008 speech at the Apostolic Church of God in Chicago) were the root causes of lower levels of Black attainment. Indeed, as Matthew Hughey notes, this interpretation was at times encouraged by Obama's own prose, which 'urges acknowledgement of "structural inequalities" alongside the belief that your "destiny is in your hands"' (2011: 21).

Yet others have argued that Obama's economically middle way and socially centrist politics led to his election, and, moreover, they can be situated within a longer lineage of African American political struggle. August Meier and Elliot Rudwick argue that the history of Black rights in America can be read as 'a slow, historical oscillation between two polarities: the impulse to integrate with the system and the urge to separate from it' (1976: 271–272). Obama's slogan 'Hope and Change' captured these tensions, embodying the belief that the racial violence and divisions of the past could be overcome and that the struggles of previous generations of activists would finally bear fruit. In short, Obama expressed the essential hope that change was possible at last. As he writes in *The Audacity of Hope*, the challenge is 'to maintain in our sights the kind of America that we want while looking squarely at America as it is, to acknowledge the sins of our past and the challenges of the present without becoming trapped in cynicism or despair' (2006: 233).

The political contexts of *Moonlight* 2: Donald Trump – the 'first white president'

The hope of the Obama years seemed to suggest that a peaceful and democratic electoral process would produce slow but concrete, socio-political change in a country riven by the effects of racism and dogged by the historical atrocity of chattel slavery and centuries of socio-political oppression of Black Americans and other ethnic minorities. However, this balance between hope and history proved difficult to sustain. From the outset of Obama's presidency, there was evidence not of the disappearance of racism but, rather, of its transfiguration and augmentation. From 2008 onward, an 'unprecedented amount of death threats against the president' were registered (Hughey, 2011: 1). Heidi Beirich and Evelyn Schlatter link a significant expansion of America's far right directly to the election of Obama: 'the election unleashed a wave of Obama-related hate crimes and domestic terrorist incidents […] Interest in joining hate and anti-government groups soared beginning in 2008' (2014: 80). Indeed, the Southern Poverty Law Center, which tracks extremist organizations in the US, noted significant rises in hate and anti-government groups after 2008: the number of hate groups rose from 602 in 2000, to 1,018 in 2011 (Beirich and Schlatter 2014: 80).

Members of the Republican Party also adopted more radical political positions. One example of this is found in the rise of the Tea Party movement, which called for less government intervention and lower taxes and led to a hardening of conservative political discourse in the country. According to Carl Pedersen, this discourse drew on 'antebellum, Civil War, and Jim Crow-era themes' (2014: 32). These themes evoke eras when the rights of African Americans were violently denied, either through the explicit legal institution of enslavement, the segregationist policies of the Southern United States, which were known as the 'Jim Crow Laws', or through the suppression of voting rights and access, which were not fully secured in law for African American men and women until the Voting Rights Act of 1965. One of the ways these Confederate-era themes are made manifest, according to Pedersen, is the so-called 'birther' movement, which suggests that Obama had been born in Kenya and was, therefore, an illegitimate president. The false rumour began in 2010 but gained traction after Donald Trump revived it on *Celebrity Apprentice* in the spring of 2011. The 'birther' lie posited Obama as a kind of 'Manchurian Candidate', one who appears to have America's best interests at heart but covertly works to bring down the federal government. In spite of the fact that Obama released his long-form birth certificate in 2011, as of August 2016, an astonishing 41% of voters who identified as Republicans disagreed with the statement 'Barack Obama was born in the United States' (Clinton and Roush 2016). Indeed, Trump's role in spreading the 'birther' falsehood provided him with a political soapbox, paving the way for his public visibility and eventual election to the presidency in 2016.

The 'birther' fabrication speaks to deeper concerns around race, class, belonging and entitlement in American political life. Philosopher George Yancy addresses these issues, considering the members of working-class, white America who voted for Trump. He states that, even as we should empathize and understand the conditions of social exclusion and economic deterioration that led many in rural 'Rust Belt' states to vote for Trump, the conditions of this vote cannot be separated from whiteness as a race category and a 'mentality'. He argues that 'even as they suffered, they always knew that they were *not* Black and thereby assumed that they were *entitled* to reap the benefits of white America' (2017: 6). Yancy cites the term 'whitelash', coined by political commentator Van Jones (Ryan 2016), as a way to understand Trump's election as president: as a response to, and a triumph over, Obama, in a country whose demographics are rapidly shifting away from a white majority.

Ta-Nehisi Coates echoes these concerns, arguing that the Obama years, when an apparent 'post-racial' America was being celebrated nationally and globally, in fact, gave new life to racist ideologies and fed deep-seated prejudices in white America (2017a). Coates calls Trump America's 'First White President', stating that the 45th president's ideology, quite simply, is white supremacy and that he is the first to make the 'awful inheritance' of slavery, racism, segregation and their attendant violence 'explicit' in his political campaigning (ibid.). If we consider the ways in which Obama embodied a triumph of the American Dream, Coates argues that Trump offers something perhaps even more appealing to his voters: 'Obama delivered to black people the hoary message that if they work twice as hard as white people, anything is possible. But Trump's counter is persuasive: Work half as hard as black people, and even more is possible' (ibid.). Radically unqualified in traditional political terms to assume the presidency, by the time of his election in November 2016, Trump was trailing a slew of sexual assault allegations and instances of sexist, racist, xenophobic, ableist and bigoted words and actions in his wake. It is possible, therefore, to conclude alongside Coates, that this was an instance of 'an American president succeeding at best in spite of his racism and possibly because of it' (ibid).

A new 'Black wave'?: Hollywood in the 2010s

Coates argues that, with hindsight, one can view the election of Obama not as the 'end of racism' and a triumph of integration but, rather, as a response to a series of crises (Hurricane Katrina, the war in Iraq, the post-9/11 security state and the 2008 financial crash) that rocked America's perception of itself as a force for good. He writes that, 'post-racialism and good feeling were taken up not so much out of elevation in consciousness but out of desperation' (2017b). The success of *Moonlight* reflects some of these tensions as well. The elevation of *Moonlight* to Oscar glory, alongside a range of critically acclaimed films by or about African Americans, can be viewed as part of the belated artistic recognition on the part of the Academy of the value of Black storytelling. However, the film can also be considered within the context of the 2016 election for which critics hailed *Moonlight* as 'essential viewing' (Ruby 2017) and 'symbolic resistance' (Devega 2016) in the age of Trump. Jenkins himself noted the increased 'urgency' of the film after the election and his hope that it may provide 'solace' to audiences (quoted in Ruby 2017). The success of *Moonlight* at this particular cultural moment speaks to Hollywood's sporadic recognition of Black and minority storytelling and as a response to a series of the industry's own crises and criticisms, including the online campaign '#OscarsSoWhite' and ongoing debates about diversity in Hollywood, in front of and behind the camera.

Debates on diversity in Hollywood are not only about the quality or quantity of filmmaking by minority groups at any given time, nor does Hollywood success represent a definitive yardstick for measuring artistic worth. What is at stake is the extent to which marginalized voices gain mainstream recognition within the predominantly white framework of the Hollywood industry. In 1968, author, activist and cultural critic James Baldwin wrote of Hollywood:

> The industry is compelled, given the way it is built, to present to the American people, a self-perpetuating fantasy of American life … And the black face, truly reflected, is not only no part of this dream, it is antithetical to it.
>
> (1968: 56)

Here, Baldwin references the ways in which Hollywood, as 'dream factory', excludes the voices of Black Americans because their stories do not fit in with the dominant narrative of the white 'American Dream'. In spite of this, in 2016–17, *Moonlight* participated in what seemed to be a long-awaited mainstream recognition of the work of Black filmmakers, actors and narratives, including Theodore Melfi's *Hidden Figures* (2016), Denzel Washington's *Fences* (2016), Jeff Nichols's *Loving* (2016), Jordan Peele's *Get Out* (2016), Dee Rees's *Mudbound* (2017), Ava DuVernay's *13th* (2016) and Raoul Peck's *I Am Not Your Negro* (2016), all of which garnered popular and critical acclaim. This group of films and filmmakers led *Guardian* critic Steve Rose to declare that Hollywood is finally acknowledging a wave of 'black talent', and he goes on to say that 'black film is rising again' (2016). The 'again' here is significant; the mid-2010s was not the first time that Hollywood congratulated itself on a 'great advance for liberal and progressive trends in American film opinion' (Guerrero 1993: 75). Hollywood has previously embraced Black filmmaking talent, most notably in the New Black Realism of the 1990s and the Blaxploitation films of the 1970s.

Debates around *Moonlight* in the film industry were also character-ized by a number of contradictions. Celebrated as a triumphal example of the entry of Black and queer lives into Hollywood, *Moonlight* also raised the issue of how many diverse filmmakers, filmmaking professionals and minority characters and narratives have been and continue to be excluded from mainstream representation. In January 2015, a controversy about diversity in Hollywood erupted following a hashtag created by April Reign, '#OscarsSoWhite'. Reign was objecting to the fact that not a single actor of colour had been included across the 20 acting nominations. In 2016, a number of high-profile Black filmmakers and stars boycotted the ceremony because of the Academy's failure to nominate a single Black actor for an award for the second year in a row. According to Ava DuVernay, whose Civil Rights-era drama *Selma* was widely believed to have been 'snubbed' by the Oscars in 2015 (Mendelson 2015), the '#OscarsSoWhite' hashtag was 'a catalyst for a conversation about what had really been a decades-long absence of diversity and inclusion' (Ugwu 2020). Indeed, no Black director has ever won a best directing Oscar – but Jenkins, Peele, Steve McQueen (*12 Years a Slave*, 2014), Lee Daniels (*Precious*, 2009) and John Singleton (*Boyz N the Hood*, 1991) have been nominated. No African American woman has ever been nominated in the same category, what Guerrero describes as a 'triple oppression' of their work, due to their race and gender, and the 'independent vision' offered by their films (1993: 174). Television, including streaming platforms, has proven to be a more accessible and diverse landscape, with shows like Justin Simien's *Dear White People* (2017), Donald Glover's *Atlanta* (2016), Issa Rae's *Insecure* (2016), Terence Nance's *Random Acts of Flyness* (2018) and Ava DuVernay's *Queen Sugar* (2016) and *When They See Us* (2019) receiving widespread audience acclaim.

Statistics on the lack of diversity in Hollywood present a startling picture of a monocultural industry in which the perspective of straight, white and males dominate, both in front of and behind the camera. Researchers at the Annenberg School for Communication and Media Diversity in Los Angeles have conducted three extensive studies on portrayals of gender, race/ethnic-ity, sexuality and disability in 2010s popular American film (Smith et al. 2014, 2015, 2016). They describe an 'epidemic of invisibility in film' in which women have less than 30% of speaking parts (2014), 74% of speak-ing parts go to white actors, while Black actors had only 4.9% of speaking parts (2016). In 2015, 66% of characters across film, television and stream-ing platforms were men and 71% white. In 2016, 76 of the top 100 films had no LGBT characters, and in the films that did feature LGBT representation, 79.1% of these characters were white. Perhaps the most startling lack of diversity was to be found behind the camera: of 900 popular films between the years 2007 and 2016, only 1.4% of films were scored by women and only 34 were directed by women, of which five were women of colour (Smith et al. 2016). Summarizing these findings, Isabel Molina-Guzmán argues that 'the reality for audiences, actors, creators, and executives of color in the entertainment industries remains defined by exclusion from the industry and invisibility on screen' (2016: 438).

Thus, in 2017, *Moonlight* seemed like a radical volte-face for an industry so long dominated by straight, white men. While *Moonlight* is certainly not the first film to represent Black, gay lives, it remains the first LGBT-themed film to win a Best Picture Oscar and to garner such mainstream plaudits. But it is important to ask why representation matters and why diverse representation in Hollywood, in particular, matters. To answer these questions, Molina-Guzmán turns to the pioneering work of cultural theorist Stuart Hall, who writes the following on race, media and representation:

> The media play a part in the formation, in the constitution, of the things that they reflect. It is not that there is a world outside, 'out there', which exits free of the discourses of representations. What is 'out there' is, in part, constituted by how it is represented.
>
> (Hall quoted in Molina-Guzmán 2014: 440)

Hall argues that media helps create the world it represents, and, in turn, the represented world influences and shapes the lives and experiences of those it depicts.

One of the most powerful and oft-cited examples of the power of film to shape public perception is that of D.W. Griffith's *The Birth of a Nation* (1915), a film that set a template for many of the damaging racist stereotypes of African Americans that would occur and recur in Hollywood films for decades (see Bogle 1994: 3–18). As Guerrero summarizes, 'the struggle over *Birth*'s racist ideology and its public exhibition signalled how deadly serious the new medium, barely twenty years old, had become as a tool to create and shape public opinion and racial perceptions' (1993: 15). The film coincided with a period when violence against African Americans was on the rise and, in the following years, the KKK reached its highest membership ever – five million. The history of *The Birth of a Nation* is a powerful reminder that, as Susan Hayward points out, in talking about race and cinema, 'one is also talking about racism and cinema's own racism' (Hayward 2006: 46). It also demonstrates the ways in which films can powerfully influence how audiences view specific groups, especially in the case of minorities, where representations may be less numerous and/or nuanced overall.

However, the capacity of film to alter perception also applies to self-perception: how it feels for marginalized groups to watch films that represent their identities. Positive representation can offer aspirations and hope to audiences, as was the case with Ryan Coogler's *Black Panther* in 2017. As the founder of the pop-culture site 'Black Girl Nerds' Jamie Broadnax notes, the characters in *Black Panther* 'are rulers of a kingdom, inventors and creators of advanced technology. We're not dealing with black pain, and black suffering […] the usual topics of acclaimed movies about the black experience' (quoted in Wallace 2018). Conversely, negative representation can entrench stereotypes and increase social marginalization: as sociologist Ronda Daniel explains, 'real-life' issues, such as police brutality and housing inequality, can be influenced by Hollywood representations because the negative depiction of young Black men 'perpetuates the idea that black incarceration rates are disproportionately high in America because "black people commit more crime"' (2017).

Increasing diversity in Hollywood, on and off screen, is a means to reflect the changing demographics of America itself. As sociologists have noted, the US is set to become a 'majority-minority' nation by the mid-twenty-first century (Pedersen 2014: 40). Changing racial and ethnic demographics in the US mean that consumers of audio-visual media are becoming more diverse than ever. Indeed, research suggests that African Americans are one of the highest consumers of representational media, historically and in the present. In the early 1970s, the Hollywood trade journal *Variety* estimated that while Black people made up 10–15% of the population, they constituted 30% of the cinema-going audience (Guerrero 1993: 83). Molina-Guzmán notes that African Americans watch movies at a greater rate than other populations and that African Americans consume more content across a wider range of platforms than any other group (2016: 442).

Given these demographics and consumption statistics, it is reasonable to ask why Hollywood continues to resist the incorporation of more diverse casts, storylines and production personnel, in contrast to trends in television. As a capitalist industry focused on profit, Hollywood is fundamentally conservative, and the 'economic risk imperative' remains an important factor in deciding whether a film gets made. There is a tension in the industry between the ongoing perception that white audiences mostly watch 'white' films, and straight audiences watch 'straight' films, and the growing reality that embracing diversity reaps economic rewards. Films by and about racial and sexual minorities are required to have 'crossover power', an appeal to white, straight and non-American audiences (see Cover 2000; Guerrero 1993: 167; Loist 2017). Additionally, as in many industries, a white-dominated workforce perpetuates itself, leading to predominantly white networks in which those who are already in the industry employ friends, colleagues and neighbours. This means that those who are, as they say, 'in the room' when decisions are made, tend to be mostly white and straight, as a few of the recent casting fiascos of white actors playing characters of colour seem to suggest (see Loreck 2018). As John D. Foster notes, such casting decisions ensure that 'whiteness remains exalted and preserved while otherness is diluted and sanitized' (2019: 173).

As the previous overview of Black filmmaking cycles in Hollywood demonstrates, the conditions under which a Black film 'wave' in Hollywood emerges exist at a complex nexus of social activism, political change and Hollywood's economic imperatives. Guerrero argues that Black films are a good investment for Hollywood – if they are made cheaply. In the 1970s, Blaxploitation films were huge commercial successes: *Sweet Sweetback's Baadasssss Song* (Van Peebles 1971), for example, cost $500,000 and made $10 million domestically within its first year of release (Guerrero 1993: 86). As further examples, he cites *New Jack City* (Van Peebles 1991), an example of New Black Realism in the 1990s, made for $8.5 million and garnering more than $47 million at the domestic box office. Similarly, *Boyz N the Hood* (Singleton 1991) cost $6 million and made nearly $57 million worldwide, an 850% profit margin. *Moonlight* operated on similarly lucrative lines: made for $1.5 million, it grossed more than $65.3 million worldwide.

Of the 1970s and 1990s, Guerrero writes, that 'expanded waves of black movie production occur in short cycles (four years or so) in an inverse relationship to the overall prosperity of the dominant film industry' (Guerrero 1993: 166). *Moonlight* premiered at the Telluride Film Festival in September 2016 and was released widely in the US in October of the same year. Indeed, if we consider Guerrero's analysis, this timing is significant, as it comes after what commentators described as the summer, and indeed the year, of the Hollywood flop. In 2016, there were '15 $100-million-plus stinkers […] twice as many as 2015' (Fritz 2016). Furthermore, many lower-budget films did not fare better: action films (*Max Steel* (Hendler)), star vehicles (*Free State of Jones* (Ross) with Matthew McConaughey), comedies (*The Brothers Grimsby* (Leterrier) and *Whiskey Tango Foxtrot* (Requa and Ficarra)), horror (*Pride and Prejudice and Zombies* (Steers)) and auteur-led, critically acclaimed dramas (*Snowden* (Stone)) all flopped at the box office (Robehmed 2016). Writing for the *Atlantic*, Derek Thompson argues that Hollywood is rapidly losing the millennial audience, who decamp to streaming platforms and social media. Hollywood's response is to churn out more and more sequels and franchises, which results in 'an increasingly expensive arms race to mint new franchises for a domestic audience that is seeking out original stuff beyond the cineplex' (2016). This context makes *Moonlight*'s commercial achievements all the more impressive and highlights the fallacies of Hollywood's 'crossover appeal' and 'economic risk aversion' strategies when it comes to diverse and independent filmmaking.

17

Conclusion: Backlash and exceptionalism

Obama, as the first Black president of the US, carried the weight of a posited and radical shift in racial attitudes in the US, one that proved to be unstable. The apparent shift toward a 'post-racial' America was radically disproven by the election of Trump, and in a similar sense, one must also remain cautious about the tendency of Hollywood and the media toward tokenism. This is when 'critical darlings', films made by or starring members of diverse communities, such as *Moonlight*, are intermittently singled out for praise. Molina-Guzmán argues that such moments, when the Academy seems on the verge of a massive cultural shift, work 'through narratives of exceptional individuals', in which 'the visibility of the exceptional few allows for the structural exclusion of the many' (2016: 443, 444). Nonetheless, the 2020 win for Korean auteur Bong Joon-ho's *Parasite* (2019) may represent a sustained move toward the recognition of diverse storytelling, a trend that appeared to carry over to the 2021 ceremony. Nominations for Chloé Zhao and Emerald Fennell (for *Nomadland* and *Promising Young Woman* respectively) produced a win for Zhao, who became the first woman of colour to win a Best Director award and only the second woman in the history of the Academy Awards since Kathryn Bigelow in 2010.

Yet, ultimately, the way Hollywood and mainstream press and audiences engage with filmmakers from diverse backgrounds must be separated from the meaning and significance of the films themselves. *Moonlight*'s recognition within the economically and socially conventional sphere of Hollywood does not necessarily undermine the film's progressive social and political aims. *Moonlight* may have been nurtured during the Obama years, but its vision is less straightforwardly optimistic about the progress of racial and sexual rights than that of the former president. As Kannan et al. note, '*Moonlight* is neither about "hope, nor change"'. They argue that, instead, *Moonlight* is a reminder that 'the representational, political, and social gains of marginalized people over recent years is not promised' (2017: 296). In the following two chapters, I will examine how *Moonlight* engages the two identities that structure the main character Chiron's experience of the world, his race and sexuality, looking also at *Moonlight*'s position within longer lineages of Black and queer filmmaking.

2 *Moonlight* and Black masculinity on screen

Moonlight speaks to a history of African American cinematic storytelling, particularly in relation to the theme of masculinity as it is explored in the film. This chapter considers stereotyping of African American men in order to examine the ways in which *Moonlight* engages with and disrupts these cinematic inheritances. The chapter also situates *Moonlight* in relation the Blaxploitation films of the 1970s and the New Black Realist films of the 1990s, examining how *Moonlight*'s depiction of Black adolescence and young adulthood converges with and diverges from these traditions. I will focus on three principal characters in the film: Chiron's mentor and father-figure Juan, Chiron's friend and love interest Kevin and, of course, Chiron himself, whose transition from boy to man the film charts. While *Moonlight* is primarily an exploration of Black masculinity, this chapter also examines the characters of Chiron's mother, Paula, and Theresa and the critical interpretations of their roles.

Masculinity and race on screen: Cinema's stereotypes

In the twentieth century, American cinema has proven to be one of the most potent and consistent means of constructing a white-dominated and stereotypical imaginary of Black people, particularly in relation to Black male characterization. Indeed, Donald Bogle, in his highly detailed history of African American representation and stereotyping on screen, argues that 'No minority was so relentlessly or fiercely typed as the black man' (1994: 17). One of the earliest and most influential examples of this false and negative stereotyping was Griffith's unabashedly racist *The Birth of a Nation*, based on the novel *The Clansman: A Historical Romance of the Ku Klux Klan* by Thomas Dixon Jr. (1905). Highly controversial at the time of its release and condemned by the NAACP (Bogle 1994: 16), the film, nonetheless, was a huge commercial success. Set in the period of Reconstruction in the Southern states after the Civil War, the film trades in

DOI: 10.4324/9780429055294-2

a number of stereotypes of African Americans that would go on to influence the portrayal of Black people on screen in the decades to come. Bogle characterizes these stereotypes as the following: 'Uncle Tom', 'coon', 'the tragic mulatto', 'mammy' and 'black buck'. He notes that 'all were character types used for the same effect: to entertain by stressing Negro inferiority' (4).

The 'black buck' stoked fears of Black male power and sexuality. As Bogle notes, these characters are depicted as 'oversexed and savage' (13). The character of Gus in *The Birth of a Nation* (played by white actor Walter Long in blackface) embodies this stereotypical character type. A former slave who has become a captain in the army, at the dramatic apogee of the film, Gus chases the white woman Flora Stoneman through a forest, where she throws herself over a cliff rather than face his advances. Other stereotypes of African American men evoked in *The Birth of a Nation* include the 'happy servant', widely known as the 'Uncle Tom', the Black man who accepts the dominance of white society, and the 'coon', usually presented as a laughing, lazy and irresponsible figure that was derived from Jim Crow-era minstrel shows. As Manthia Diawara summarizes, *The Birth of a Nation* 'created and fixed an image of Blackness that was necessary for racist America's fight against Black people' (1993: 3).

Ed Guerrero writes that, with *The Birth of a Nation*, images of Black people as 'infantile, lazy and subservient', dominant in the Jim Crow-era, 'are supplemented with the radically newer images of blacks as vicious beasts and rapists' (1993: 12). These images were not confined to the silent era: they have been repeated and reworked across a range of media through the twentieth and twenty-first centuries.

Stereotyping of African Americans is extensive, and Ronald Jackson outlines the 'nineteen character-types' based upon racist depictions, including: 'the savage African, the happy slave, the devoted servant, the corrupt politician, the irresponsible citizen, the petty thief, the social delinquent, the vicious criminal, the sexual superman, the superior athlete, the unhappy non-white, the natural-born cook, the natural-born musician' (2006: 24). As Bogle notes, such stereotypes function to sustain an image of Black inferiority; Richard Dyer reiterates this notion, arguing that 'stereotyping […] is one of the means by which [oppressed groups] are categorized and kept in their place' (1997: 12). Stereotypes thrive on distance and lack of knowledge of the stereotyped individual or group: when one has intimate or even proximate knowledge of that person or group, it is more difficult to sustain easy and shallow mischaracterizations about their behaviours, beliefs and identities. In this vein, bell hooks calls stereotypes 'fictions', arguing that 'they are there not to tell it like it is but to invite and encourage pretense.

They are a fantasy, a projection onto the Other that makes them less threatening' (hooks 2015: 170).

In relation to depictions of Black men on screen, Robyn Weigman argues these contradictory tensions exist within the stereotype, oscillating 'between feminization (buffoonish Uncle Tom) and hypermasculinization (well-endowed rapist)' (1993: 180). Indeed, if we consider Jackson's categorizations, apparent contradictions emerge: the threatening 'criminal' or 'delinquent' is at odds with the 'devotion' of the servant or the affability of the musician. These contradictions lie at the heart of the stereotype, and they may, as hooks notes, make the 'Other' less threatening, but they also serve to reinforce the difference and inferiority of the stereotyped individual in relation to the assumed ideal of a white norm. Homi K. Bhabha addresses what he calls the 'ambivalence' of the racial stereotype, noting that stereotypes must perform a contradictory dance of simultaneously affirming the similarity *and* difference of the stereotyped Other. The object of stereotype cannot be too different to the self, otherwise the fear would be too great – how, then, could the object of the stereotype be controlled and understood? At the same time, this difference to self and the implied inferiority must be absolutely maintained and affirmed in order to legitimize racial exploitation. This is why stereotypes of African Americans in film encompass both the fearful and the foolish: stereotypes must retain familiarity in order to be legible while also preserving distance and difference (Bhabha 2009: 145–71). In the following section, I look at the representation of Black masculinity in the 'hood' films that primarily constitute what Diawara calls 'New Black Realism' (1993: 23) and touch on the Blaxploitation films of the 1970s. This will trace the figure of youthful Black masculinity on screen and offer a point of comparison with *Moonlight* in terms of their negotiation of histories of racist and stereotypical representation.

Blaxploitation and New Black Realism

Guerreros's expansive study of Black representation in Hollywood tracks the intersecting social and cultural conditions that led to the emergence of Blaxploitation and New Black Realism in Hollywood. He argues that the Blaxploitation movement was a response to the 'surge in African American identity politics' in the 1960s and 1970s, which included the Black Power movement, Marxism and Black nationalism (1993: 69–71). In the early 1970s, three major films were produced by Black directors: Gordon Parks Jr.'s *Super Fly* (1972), Gordon Parks Sr., *Shaft* (1971) and Melvin Van Peebles's *Sweet Sweetback's Baadasssss Song* (1971). The films were set in Northern cities, and they combined a strong social consciousness with fast-paced action sequences featuring sex, drugs and violence, alongside critically acclaimed soul and funk soundtracks. Guerrero also suggests that Blaxploitation films were a response to repeated racist stereotypes of African Americans found in decades of Hollywood filmmaking, as well as to a fatigue among Black audiences with Sidney Poitier's star persona as an embodiment of respectability politics (1993: 73). Playing characters that were middle-class, highly educated and well mannered, the Poitier figure fought racism by good example.

By contrast, the figure of masculinity that emerged in Blaxploitation films was an outlaw, a man who recognized that the law was the enemy of the Black community. Jackson argues that the figure of the 'Buck' was prominent in the Blaxploitation films of the 1970s. The 'Buck' character is a physically strong, sometimes violent and/or criminal 'sexual superman' (Jackson 2006: 24). Thus, Jackson describes *Shaft* as 'a macho-rigid Black detective who magnetized and mesmerized beautiful women by his evident strength, unquestionable fortitude, and role as hero and savior of the community' (43). Yet, it is important to note the distinction here between the stereotype of the 'Buck' as represented by white Hollywood and its reworking in Blaxploitation films (particularly those by Black directors). The positive aspects of the stereotype are emphasized, and the powerful Black man, in this case, works on behalf of the community to improve their situation rather than merely being violent or criminal as an end in itself. This is the distinction that John W. Roberts draws between 'bad man' and 'baaad man' characters. He argues that the former commits crimes for selfish gains, while the latter is a Robin Hood figure who breaks rules to challenge white supremacy and fight for his community (1989: 171–220).

While Blaxploitation films were infused with the soul and funk music of the era, the New Black Realism films of the 1990s, also called 'hood' films, capture the importance of hip-hop culture to the 1990s. Notable examples of these films include Singleton's *Boyz N the Hood*, Mario Van Peebles *New Jack City* (1991) and the Hughes brothers' *Menace II Society* (1993). Sharing some the themes of Blaxploitation films, New Black Realism films are often darker in tone, capturing the fallout from Ronald Reagan's 'war on drugs' and focusing on gang violence and urban degeneration in America's large cities, primarily Los Angeles. The social context of the two film waves also differs significantly. While Blaxploitation came out of militant political activism of Civil Rights movement, the films of the 1990s arose out of despair at ongoing political and social deprivation and segregation of African Americans in cities and the punitive policies enacted in the 'war on drugs'. Guerrero notes that these films capture the growing realization on the part of the Black middle class that 'success [has] not delivered them from the insults and isolation of a persistent and growing racism' (1993: 159).

As the moniker 'New Black Realism' would suggest, these films are based in real-world locations and communities with an emphasis on the concrete challenges faced by individuals who live there. The films treat the theme of violence within the Black community, moving beyond simplistic notions of 'Black on Black crime' (Braga and Brunson 2015). Instead, many of these films seek to foreground the social causes of crime and violence, with some, like *Boyz N the Hood*, offering semi-didactic narratives that create awareness and posit solutions. Like Blaxploitation, and unlike the blockbusters of the 1980s that paired prominent Black actors (such as Eddie Murphy) with white stars, these films feature predominantly Black casts and are produced and directed by predominantly Black crews. In these films, Diawara writes that white people are 'marginalized', with 'Black people [...] neither marginalized as a problem, nor singled out as villainous stereotypes' (1993: 7). For the most part, New Black Realist films adopt the realist conventions of classical Hollywood storytelling. They have linear narratives with a focus on a primary protagonist and what Diawara calls the 'quest for the formation of the family and individual freedom' (1993: 11). Like *Moonlight,* many are coming-of-age dramas in which young male characters are confronted by a complex web of drugs and gang violence in narratives that centre on '(re)gaining manhood for black men' (Walcott 2003: 57). The male protagonist or group of protagonists navigate gender norms, racism, violence and sexuality in their passage to adulthood.

For example, *Boyz N the Hood* begins in childhood and tracks the fortunes of Tre Styles and his friends Ricky and Doughboy, who all chose different paths in their journey to maturity. The '(re)gaining of manhood' captured in these films offers a few pathways, encapsulated in the characters in *Boyz N the Hood*: fatherhood and/or leadership in the community (the character of Furious Styles, Tre's father), leaving and gaining an education (Ricky and Tre) or staying and joining one of the gangs, where masculinity is bound up in violence, criminality and the denigration of Black women (Doughboy). As Michael Eric Dyson notes in his reading of *Boyz N the Hood*, 'black men turn to black women as scapegoats for their oppression, lashing out – often with physical violence – at those closest to them' (1992: 124). Indeed, these films have been critiqued by a number of feminist scholars for the use of misogynistic and homophobic language (Jones 1991: 32; hooks 2015: 109; Bausch 2013: 274).

At the same time, the New Black Realist films do offer many nuanced explorations of the community they depict, as well as strong anti-violence messages. Many point to the struggles of Black women while also depicting stereotypes, a tension I return to at the end of this chapter in relation to *Moonlight.* For example, *Boyz N the Hood* contrasts Tre's mother's impassioned speech about the role of Black mothers in raising children with the negative depiction of neglectful or addicted mothers. The films also critique a culture that glorifies and reproduces violence, and the ending of *Boyz N the Hood* is a case in point. Doughboy, a gang member and a caring brother and friend, laments that while the news reports on violence in foreign countries, nothing is shown of the gang violence that exists within the borders of the city of Los Angeles or America itself. As he opines, 'either they don't know, don't show, or don't care about what's going on in the hood'. This highlights the great significance of these films: they brought visibility the characters and widespread awareness to the complexity of the social worlds that they navigate. As Diawara notes, the 'the dispute over the control of the hood is also a dispute over images' (1993: 22), and in controlling the images produced about their own communities, filmmakers of the New Black Realist movement sought to shift mainstream debate away from the dehumanizing rhetoric of Reagan's policies. Ultimately, as Dyson argues, *Boyz N the Hood* 'transcends insular preoccupations with "positive" or "negative" images and instead presents at once the limitations and virtues of black culture' (1992: 127).

Characterization and masculinity in *Moonlight*

Moonlight might also be said to present the 'virtues and limitations', not of Black culture itself, but of how it is presented on screen. The film evokes some common representational and thematic stereotypes, such as drug use and drug dealing, frequent physical violence perpetrated by and against young Black boys and men and homophobia within the Black community. Referencing these issues, Kannan et al. suggest that '*Moonlight* trades on many of the tried-and-true narratives of the supposed natural and cultural dysfunction of the African American "experience"' (2017: 289). Some of the characters in the film, such as Juan, Paula and, eventually, Chiron himself, could be said to conform to well-worn and gendered cinematic stereotypes of African Americans in film: 'the drug dealer', 'the crack-addicted mother'. However, in the following section, I consider the ways in which *Moonlight* conjures up these familiar filmic tropes but also undermines and renders them complex through nuanced characterization, leading to a text that, according to several critics, ultimately 'avoids clichés of poor black narratives' (Zaman 2016: 42) and 'eschews the clichés that seem to adhere in the film's subject matter' (Allen 2017: 627).

If Dyer argued that going against stereotype was a way for audiences to feel as though a film was 'getting real' (1997: 12), *Moonlight* goes a long way toward reconfiguring stereotypes of Black manhood, 'revel[ling] in the complexity and multiplicity of black masculinities' (Kannan et al. 2017: 293). The opening scenes of the film demonstrate the film's engagement

Figure 2.1 Juan's first appearance in the film.

with, and undermining of, cinematic stereotypes of Black masculinity on screen. The character of Juan is presented initially as the epitome of the 'Black urban drug dealer', whose style and swagger open the film (see Figure 2.1). Juan can, thus, be linked to the 'bad man' characters of the Blaxploitation genre as a tough, normatively masculine outlaw. Juan's position as a high-level drug dealer in the community is made evident in the scene when he chastises one of his street dealers for selling too publicly. As previously mentioned, Roberts's exploration of these 'bad man' characters draws distinctions between the 'bad' man and what William L. Van Deburg (2014: 68) describes as a 'social bandit', a person who is 'bad for a good reason', such as challenging white supremacist violence.

Yet, Jenkins and McCraney complicate the distinction between these figures in several ways by sketching a Juan that is neither as firmly righteous as someone like Furious Styles in *Boyz N the Hood* nor as selfishly infamous as Nino Brown in *New Jack City*. Juan's first encounter with the young Chiron shows a tender, generous and humorous side, as he follows Chiron into an abandoned building where he has been chased by a group of boys. Juan quite literally opens a window into and onto Chiron's world and takes him to a diner for something to eat. This is one of several sequences in which Chiron is fed by men in his life and can be linked to the final scene of the film when Chiron reunites with Kevin, and they share a meal. Food and its association with comfort and care are, thus, immediately linked to the character of Juan, who is frequently shot at the same level as Chiron, demonstrating the ways in which he seeks to position himself as a companion and equal to the boy. At the same time, Juan is in a morally ambiguous position because he deals drugs to Chiron's mother Paula, and as Paula's addiction worsens, the time that Chiron spends with Juan and his partner Theresa increases.

The theme of male mentorship, fathers and father-figures is also present in *Boyz N the Hood*; as Guerrero notes, that film centres these relationships to such a degree that 'all these young men's futures turn on the absence or presence of fathers' (Guerrero 1993: 185). Juan's role in Chiron's life counters stereotypes of Black men as indifferent carers to children, even as the absence of Chiron's biological father seems to reinforce these stereotypes. The character of Juan is based on a real-life father figure for McCraney, a man called Blue who cared for him when he was growing up:

> Blue was the first man in his life who really looked out for him, the first man he could look up to. Blue taught him to ride a bike, took him to the ocean, held him as he learned to swim, made him feel like he might have a place in the world after all.
>
> (Adams 2017)

One weekend, having been away, McCraney returned home to find Blue missing: he had been killed, and McCraney remembers time stopping at this moment, and he thought: 'This is a very strong lesson for you. The good things in your life are not always' (quoted in Adams 2017). Just as Blue supported McCraney, Juan is kind to Chiron, and the older man's influence seems to permeate through the young man's life. Juan rejects the homophobic slurs directed toward the boy, instead offering him a model of gentle and benevolent acceptance. When Chiron, with hints of both naiveté and premature knowledge, asks Juan 'what's a faggot?', the older man replies, 'You can be gay, but ... you don't have to let nobody call you a faggot'. This distinction between the fact, or possibility, of being gay and the derogatory term 'faggot' marks Juan as compassionate and open-minded, which is particularly significant within the context of the 1980s.

Juan demonstrates keen sensitivity to the differences between how one appears in the world and how one views oneself – how we see ourselves and how others see us. Indeed, in Juan's role as mentor and father figure, one of the great lessons that he transmits to Chiron is that of self-actualization, of determining one's own path in life. At the beach, Juan tells Chiron a story about an old woman in Cuba who told him that, under moonlight, 'black boys look blue'. This is a key concept and phrase in the film, and I will return to other readings of its meaning throughout this book. However, one interpretation relates to this notion of a gap between internal self-perception and the exterior that others discern. Moonlight might change the boy's appearance to look blue to an observer, but he remains Black to himself. This meaning is further enhanced by Juan's assertion that 'At some point you gotta decide for yourself who you gonna be. Can't let nobody make that decision for you'. The previous scene in which Juan teaches Chiron to swim, encouraging him to float, further enhances the meaning of this phrase, as Juan reassures Chiron, saying 'I got you, I got you'. The implication here is that growth – personhood – comes from both letting go – floating, being yourself – while also being supported.

The film's central study in terms of Black masculinity is, of course, the character of Chiron. This study evolves over the three acts that structure the film in which Chiron moves from childhood, to adolescence, to adulthood in sections that are titled 'I – Little', 'II – Chiron' and 'III – Black'. One of the many bittersweet moments in *Moonlight*'s narrative is that by the third act, Juan's parable of colour under moonlight, and his exhortation that Chiron create his own identity, appears to not have transpired: Chiron has let his environment change him. In Chapter 5, I return to the image of Black boyhood presented in the first act, but in this section, I consider the representation of Chiron's adolescence and adulthood. *Moonlight* self-reflectively focuses not only on the image of Black masculinity as expressed externally but also on the performance of Black male identity as socially inflected performance. Jenkins shows how the performative construction of masculinity begins in childhood and adolescence, and he writes that 'the world is always projecting this idea of who a black man is while there is always the performance of black masculinity' (quoted in Boyce Gillespie 2017: 56).

Chiron's adolescence is marked by the absence of Juan. An important presence in the first section of the film, Juan is no longer in Chiron's life by Part II, an absence that remains unexplained. This is one of several instances in which the viewer fills in the narrative ellipses of the film, and one might assume that Juan has been killed. The fact that this death takes place off screen, in contrast to the violent and heartrending murders depicted in a film like *Boyz N the Hood*, is characteristic of *Moonlight*'s overall focus on depicting events in a minor rather than a major key. The loss of his mentor, therefore, is the structuring absence that marks Chiron as teenager. The other major change in Chiron's life is his mother's worsening addiction, which sees him escape to the quiet of Theresa's house.

Like other coming-of-age films, the relation of the individual to their peer group assumes particular importance in the narrative, relationships that are navigated in the key sites of school and neighbourhood. In Chiron's case, there are many factors that mark him as different. Firstly, teenage Chiron is depicted as a gawky, awkward kid, with arms and legs that appear too long for his body (see Figure 2.2). His scrawniness is emphasized by trousers that are slightly too short, a fact that the neighbourhood bullies do not fail to pick up on. These bullies, led by the particularly cruel but also insightful Terrel, mock him for his clothes, his appearance, his mother's addiction and for being gay. Bullying most often takes place when there is difference and when a person is perceived as an outsider to a group. Chiron's

Figure 2.2 Chiron depicted as an awkward teenager.

homosexuality is barely perceived and as yet unexplored by him, but others sense this difference, an experience that has been cited as fairly common among queer youth and that McCraney describes as the community 'know[ing] things about him before he knows them about himself' (quoted in Walker 2017). This is a quite literal rendering of Juan's exhortation that Chiron does not 'let others tell you who you gonna be': the bullies are quite literally telling Chiron who and what he is, and, therefore, it is perhaps unsurprising that when we meet Chiron the adult, he has rejected or suppressed the queer elements of his identity.

In their ability to understand the social codes that make them don the correct clothes and assume the right posturing, the bullies might be said to be adopting what Richard Majors calls the 'cool pose'. Majors describes this pose as arising from the structural violence and oppression imposed on Black men in white-dominated society, whereby 'this particular attitude and behaviour represents for them their best safeguard against further mental or physical abuse' (Majors quoted in hooks 2015: 111). Coates links the posturing of characters like Terrel to fear: 'the crews walked the blocks of their neighbourhood, loud and rude, because it was only through their loudness and rudeness that they might feel any sense of security and power' (2015: 22). Indeed, *Moonlight* offers a glimpse under the performative mask of even nasty characters like Terrel. Without offering Terrel any backstory, the film's general focus on the performance of masculinity invites a questioning of the world in which such displays of aggression are not only tolerated but accepted and even rewarded.

Moonlight also explores the performance of this kind of sexualized, faux-aggressive masculinity through the character of Kevin. We first encounter the teenage Kevin in a corner hallway in the school, where he elaborates a detailed and possibly hyperbolic account of a sexual encounter with a girl. There is foreshadowing and irony as Kevin says that he is telling Chiron the story because 'I know you can keep a secret'; irony because this is very obviously a story that Kevin wants to be told and foreshadowing because it precedes Kevin and Chiron's sexual encounter on the beach, which, by dint of its homosexuality, must remain a secret. That night, Chiron has a vivid dream in which he watches Kevin and the girl have intense, noisy penetrative sex, during which Kevin turns to look Chiron directly in the eye. This scene captures something essential about Chiron, a repeating pattern throughout the film: the sense that he is a watcher or viewer in his own life (see Chapter 3).

Coming-of-age dramas are often marked by impulses of freedom and containment: characters are caught between the relative liberty of childhood and burgeoning adult responsibility, which remains a responsibility to yet be fully assumed. Indeed, Karen Lury describes the process by which children in films move into adolescence as one of tethering, being brought down to earth (2018). Such tensions between freedom and constraint are further heightened by the materiality of the lives at stake. If, for example, one examines a coming-of-age drama, such as *Stand By Me* (Reiner, 1986) or *Boyhood*, the 'tethering', or increasing assumption of adult knowledge and responsibility, comes about through interpersonal drama and crisis, such as the death of a relative or friend. However, within the context of a deprived urban area such as that of Liberty City, constraint is already part of the material fabric of the built environment. In *Moonlight*, Jenkins captures the sense of confinement in Liberty City in the mid-section of the film through a focus on wire, walls, fences, washing lines, doors and other barriers that frequently impede Chiron's physical progress through the space (see Figure 2.3).

Yet Chiron does find release, centred on one of the most poignant sequences of the film, a scene centred on touch. Chiron stays out all night, perhaps to avoid Paula, and travels on lonely trains to get to the beach in Central Miami, which is deserted at that time of night. Like many narrative actions in *Moonlight*, Chiron's choice of location for this night flight is left unspoken, but it is possible to infer that he is returning to a place that reminds him of Juan. There, he encounters Kevin, who immediately invites Chiron to drop any pretence of toughness, saying 'why you pretendin'? You puttin' on a show for me Black'? One of Kevin's great qualities is this ability to pierce through Chiron's exterior presentation of self, but his words also ring true for himself. Perhaps this is what allows Kevin to survive and navigate his world with apparently more success than Chiron: his acute awareness of role-playing, the times when one can drop or assume the exterior mask, allows him to retain a strong sense of self.

Figure 2.3 The confinement of Liberty City depicted through the image of Chiron fenced in at school.

Chiron's attempt to put up a front with Kevin, as he says, 'I ain't no boy', is firmly but kindly dismantled by Kevin, who responds, 'the hell you ain't'. This might be read as Kevin gently teasing Chiron for his posited weakness in comparison to the other teenagers, but it is also an invitation for Chiron to accept and, perhaps, even embrace his own vulnerability. This sense of a recognition and beauty that can be found in release, in letting oneself trust and be vulnerable to another's touch, is visualized when the boys share a delicate kiss and an onanistic and oneiric moment together (see Figure 2.4). Forms of touch are highlighted in this sequence, from what is not visualized of the boys' pleasurable masturbation, to what is given an

Figure 2.4 Kevin and Chiron kiss on the beach.

image, Chiron's hand coiling delicately in the sand. Yet a subsequent scene shows how swiftly tender touch can turn to violence, as Kevin is forced by the school bullies to beat Chiron. These scenes, moving so quickly from the touch of pleasure and care to the touch that hurts, recall Judith Butler's assertion that:

> The body implies mortality, vulnerability, agency: the skin and the flesh expose us to the gaze of others, but also to touch, and to violence, and bodies put us at risk of becoming the agency and instrument of all these as well.
>
> (2004: 26)

The physical, sexual and emotional freedom that Chiron experiences with Kevin is fleeting, and the images of containment described above reach their apogee when Terrel and the others force Kevin to beat Chiron, as they stand around him in a circle (see Figure 2.5). Thus, *Moonlight* shows the ways in which social context renders some bodies more vulnerable to violence. Kevin is conscripted into this pattern of abuse and forced to hit and betray his friend in order to retain his status and his own safety. As he beats Chiron, Kevin quietly begs his friend to 'stay down, stay down', another example of Kevin's awareness of role-playing: he is inviting Chiron to perform submission. Chiron does not, and this puts another cast on Kevin's ability to perform and integrate when fitting in means betraying those you care about.

The school system offers little in the way of either succour or justice for Chiron. For example, the school's guidance counsellor chides Chiron after Terrel and the others beat him, saying that 'if you were a man it'd be

Figure 2.5 Terrel and the other bullies force Kevin to beat Chiron.

four other knuckleheads sitting right there with you', implying that Chiron's nonviolence equates with a lack of manliness. Perhaps Chiron's refusal to 'stay down' is a manifestation of Juan's exhortation to him to not let anyone define who he will be. Yet, this beating results in a retaliatory gesture that lands Chiron in prison, and one might consider to what extent gestures of emancipatory self-actualization can apply in a white supremacist society that constructs Black people, particularly young Black men, as criminal. Philosopher George Yancy argues that, in North America, 'from the perspective of whiteness, the Black body is criminality itself' (Yancy 2016: xvi). Unlike *Boyz N the Hood*, in which the representatives of the flawed school system are white, it is worth noting that the teacher in this case is Black. This lends credence to the charge that *Moonlight* can be construed as a film about 'racism without racists': the effects of racism are visualized but embodied in Black characters.

However, perhaps this tacit acceptance on the part of the representative of the school highlights the ways in which, for young people of colour, the school system is failing systemically and not only on the basis of the individual. Studies show that 'predominantly non-White schools are more than 1,000% more likely to have concentrated levels of poverty among their students', while teachers do not expect the same levels of attainment from Black and Hispanic children as white or Asian students (Hughey 2011: 15–16). Indeed, Coates argues that the school system is an early means of learning the violent disciplining of the body. He suggests that for Black youth, 'fear and violence' are the 'weaponry' of the school system, whereby 'those who failed in the schools justified their destruction in the streets. The society could say, "He should have stayed in school", and then wash its hands of him' (2015: 33).

Statistics surrounding the disciplinary procedures of the school system paint a grim picture of what has been dubbed the 'school to prison pipeline'. Black students are three times more likely to be suspended and expelled than white students, while Black students represent 31% of school-related arrests. Since the 1970s, there has been a 600% rise in the number of people incarcerated in US, and young black men have a 28% chance of incarceration over their lifetime. The chance of going to prison among young Black men rises to 50% among high school dropouts (Hughey 2001: 18; Crawley and Hirschfeld 2018). In *Moonlight*, the school does little to stem the tide of bullying against Chiron, and when he eventually retaliates through a use of force that the school counsellor subtly deemed necessary, he is carried off in a police car. This scene closes the second act of the film and appears to be an echo of *Boyz N the Hood*, whose own first act closes with the child character of Doughboy being carried away in a police car.

The third section of the film bears witness to Chiron's adulthood, and it is titled 'III - Black', the nickname that Kevin gave him. The opening shots in this section present a physically transformed character, suggesting that the moment he was pushed into the police car was an instance of burgeoning adulthood when he decided he would no longer be 'Chiron', a vulnerable young person who could be the target of violence. Black, as we meet him in Act III of the film, creates an effect of power that recalls much of Juan's style: he wears a thick gold chain, diamond earrings, gold caps on his teeth and a gun nestled like a talisman in the passenger seat of the car (see Figure 2.6). Like Juan, he also has a plastic crown air freshener on the dashboard. Rap booms from the speakers of his car, similarly to how Juan was introduced by a strong musical cue. But while Juan's 1970s soul brought a nostalgic, mostly uplifting mood to the opening scene, the track that plays when Chiron is introduced is Atlanta rap group Goodie Mob's 'Cell Therapy' (1994). This dark, dystopian song deals with American violence at home and abroad and touches on themes of gentrification, Black incarceration, US domestic and foreign policy, martial law and concentration camps.

However, as previously mentioned, Jenkins's focus in *Moonlight* is not on Black masculinity in and of itself but, rather, on the performance of Black masculinity, and it is in Section III that the gap between reality and performance comes most into focus. As Butler demonstrates, gender itself is performative – gender is a repetition of the acts associated with masculinity and/or femininity; 'gender is not a fact, and the various acts of gender create the idea of gender' (2006: 190). These acts, these scripts of gender, were already 'in place', repeated and recognized by society, before any one individual begins to assume them. As she writes, 'the act that one does, the act that one performs is, in a sense, an act that's been going on before

Figure 2.6 Chiron as Black, recalling much of Juan's style.

one arrived on the scene' (1988: 526). Jenkins carefully underscores the distinction between Black's interior and exterior presentation as a means to highlight this performative aspect of gender. Therefore, before we witness Black as he presents himself to the world, Act III begins with a dream sequence. Paula appears against the backdrop of the pink and green tones of their old apartment, shot in a low angle as from the perception of the child Chiron as she screams at him. This is followed by an abrupt cut to the adult Black, waking in his bed gasping and sweating, shaken by this night vision. This transitions to a scene in a bathroom where the syncopated rhythm of the opening bars of 'Cell Therapy' begins to play. Shot with a stark, electric, blue-green light, the image shows Chiron's back as he dips his face into a sink filled with ice cubes and water.

This scene and the sound of 'Cell Therapy' acts as a bridge between the interiority of the dream sequence and subsequent waking. It highlights how Black assumes the mantle that he expresses to the world in stages, from dreaming as a frightened young boy, to moving into the world as a man who inspires fear in others. This makes *Moonlight* a particular kind of coming-of-age movie, one in which the vicissitudes and torments of adolescence do not end in resolution at the end of the film, but instead, the viewer sees how these pains write themselves on the adult body. The scene also demonstrates the ways in which bodies change in response to violence. The body that is subjected to violence does not remain the same, internally or externally. Roxanne Gay eloquently expresses this sentiment in writing about her experience of rape: 'The past is written on my body. I carry it every single day. The past sometimes feels like it might kill me. It is a very heavy burden' (2017: 37). Chiron's transformation of his body as well as of his style, clothing and accessories recalls Coates's description of the young men in his own neighbourhood in Baltimore, whose exterior presentation of a threatening masculinity belies their underlying fear and vulnerability to violence: 'the fear was there in the extravagant boys of my neighborhood, in their large rings and medallions, their big puffy coats and full-length fur-collared leathers, which was their armor against the world' (2015: 14). Chiron was hurt very badly for appearing weak, so he transforms himself into Black, a physically and socially powerful man.

The re-naming of Chiron to Black also has several possible significations: it suggests that Chiron is adopting a persona, one that draws strength from a Black political and social identity, and it hints at the ongoing importance of Kevin's friendship to Chiron, for it was Kevin who first called Chiron by the nickname. It also returns us symbolically to Juan's phrase, one that echoes through the film, 'in moonlight black boys look blue'. If this can be read as Juan's exhortation to Chiron to not let others define his identity, then the presentation of the adult Black suggests that Juan's advice has not been followed: Black has been influenced by the violence he experienced, becoming, as far as possible, invulnerable. The physical invulnerability he appears to strive for is mirrored in an apparent emotional closure. Paula begs him to remember that 'your heart ain't gotta be black like mine', introducing the idea of blackness as a colour associated with injury – one might imagine a heart that is charred by repeatedly being held too close to the flames of suffering.

Thus, we can problematize Juan's advice that Chiron not 'let anyone tell you who you gonna be', and ask along with Janine Jones, to what extent such individual self-actualization is possible within the white supremacist structure of the Black ghetto (Jones 2019; Wacquant 2010)? To what extent can Chiron truly realize his full potential given the limitations imposed on him by the racist, homophobic structures of American society? Even Juan, who first exhorted Chiron to follow his own path, did not choose his own fate. In this sense, *Moonlight* poses some of the dilemmas raised by films like *Boyz N the Hood* in which only the individuals who leave succeed; others die, or remain, but the segregation stays in place, and the hood remains unreformed. As Kenneth Chan points out about *Boyz N the Hood*, 'the film appears to walk the tightrope of critiquing racism in society and, at the same time, proposing personal accountability as the flip side of the coin' (1998: 41).

In a similar sense, *Moonlight* risks becoming a 'a film about "racism without racists", about heteronormativity without homophobes, and about oppression without oppressors' (Kannan et al. 2017: 291). The roots of Chiron's problems (racism, poverty, housing inequality, drug policies) remain explicitly unaddressed. While *Moonlight* is rightly lauded for its all-Black cast, the exclusion of whiteness also means that the problems of Liberty City remain in Liberty City, and the viewer gains little sense of the wider structural inequities that have contributed to Chiron's situation. Jones argues that many viewers 'co-create' this missing background, filling in these gaps with their own knowledge of racism, homophobia, the war on drugs, urban ghettoization and the school to prison pipeline; nonetheless, the risk remains that the viewer who is not aware of this wider social context might miss these deeper structural causes (2019: 94–7).

However, one redeeming factor for *Moonlight* is that, unlike the character of Tre from *Boyz N the Hood*, who at the end of the film appears to achieve personal fulfillment through flight from South Central and the socially sanctioned route of university (Chan 1998: 41), *Moonlight* does not offer an escape route that comes from wider society for Chiron; instead, the film tentatively places the possibility of redemption in the people of Liberty City. Transformation in the film begins with interpersonal connection, with the sharing of vulnerability, a choice that leaves

Jenkins's work open to the charge of ignoring the structural dimensions of inequality, but one that also places an emphasis on regeneration within and through the Black community. The seeds of Chiron's possible renewal lie in relationships: his reconnection with Kevin, the tentative reparation of his ties to Paula and the memory of the love and acceptance he received from Juan and Teresa. Having considered *Moonlight*'s largely positive reappraisal of Black male stereotypes, the final section examines one of the most obvious and enduring stereotypes featured in *Moonlight*, that of Chiron's mother, Paula.

Representing women in *Moonlight*

In relation to gender and stereotype, the representation of Paula has been a source of scrutiny and critique. Paula is a mother and a drug addict, a familiar gendered stereotype in 1980s and 1990s film, a period coinciding with the crack epidemic in the United States. This stereotype appears in a number of films, including those of New Black Realist directors. As Kimberly Springer notes, 'the image of the welfare queen morphed into the crack-addicted mother, who became a mainstay of late 1980s and 1990s political rhetoric linking race and gender to the war on drugs' (2007: 254). For many critics, Paula represents a damaging reiteration of a common stereotype; as R. Boylorn of the Crunk Feminist Collective writes, '"Bad" black mamas are common tropes in films where black women are scapegoated, in Moynihan fashion, as the precursor for pathology in the black family' (2016). Referencing a 1965 policy paper that argued that the rise in single-parent Black families was not due to poverty but rather so-called 'ghetto culture', Boylorn here suggests that the 'bad' Black mother stereotype in film is as anti-feminist and racially biased as this widely lambasted document.

In *Moonlight*, another issue in relation to gendered stereotyping in the film is the stark opposition drawn between angry, addicted Paula and caring, reliable Teresa. For Boylorn, 'they are diametrically oppositional characters. One breaks Chiron, the other one mends him' (2016). Indeed, Jarod Sexton connects Teresa (and Juan) to saints, Juan de la Cruz and Teresa de Jesús, both of whom emphasized the importance of faith and good works to salvation and were lambasted by the patriarchal Church fathers for this reason (2017: 175). Thus, when Chiron visits Theresa in her quiet home with its neutral beige and white tones, he goes to bed early, drinks water with his dinner and she gently teaches him how to make the bed. In a subsequent sequence, he encounters Paula in the harsh bright light of morning as she approaches him, apparently wheedling for money. A close up of Paula's face, combined with a desynchronized soundtrack and a lens that shifts in and out of focus, captures both Paula's disorientation and Chiron's as he struggles to keep up with the vagaries of her shifting mood, which oscillates between placatory coaxing and spiteful anger. Later, Chiron comes home to find her passed out on the couch, and he places a blanket over her sleeping form. Thus, while Teresa cares for Chiron and settles him for sleep, it is he who puts Paula to bed.

Kannan et al. argue that *Moonlight* 'construct[s] gender as a zero-sum relation, whereby female agency and nuance are sacrificed on the altar of diverse representations of masculinity' (2017: 293). It is certainly true that *Moonlight* focuses on Black masculinity, and the same might be said for Jenkins's other feature films, *Medicine for Melancholy* and *If Beale Street Could Talk*. Although each of these films is ostensibly about a couple, the male character in each case is the more nuanced and developed of the two. In *Medicine for Melancholy*, for example, while Jo dates a white man and wears a Barbara Loden T-shirt, it is Micah who appears to initiate her somewhat into San Francisco's Black cultural scene when they visit the Museum of the African Diaspora in San Francisco. *If Beale Street Could Talk* invites the viewer to see the male character Fonny through the eyes of his girlfriend Tish, as well as offering an extended, tense sequence in which their friend describes his experience of being wrongly incarcerated. Perhaps Micah's words in *Medicine for Melancholy* summarize Jenkins's approach: 'I'm a Black man. That's how I see myself and how the world sees me'. Actor Stephen James, who plays Fonny, reiterates this focus: 'historically there's been a limited perspective on what black masculinity looks like, what the black male looks like [...] Barry is sort of radical in that sense; he challenges perspectives' (quoted in Bradbury 2019).

Of course, a focus on masculinity does not necessarily imply that femininity must be 'sacrificed'. Indeed, other critics have viewed the representation of Paula in more nuanced terms, suggesting that her character can be read beyond the stereotype. Naomi Harris, the actor who plays Paula, was initially reluctant to take on the role because of its negative and clichéd connotations. She researched the character by watching YouTube documentaries about Miami in the 1980s and crack addiction. She came to understand Paula as someone who was coping, alone, with the pain of addiction: as she notes, '[Paula] was never given the love that she needed, so with an empty tank, how can you fill somebody else's?' (quoted in McDonald 2016). For some critics, Paula is less a fully formed character than an overwhelming presence in her son's life. In this sense, as Francey Russell argues, Paula is a character 'refracted through Chiron's memory, fantasy, and experience' (2016). The use of audio-visual anti-realist techniques, such as stark reds and pinks and desynchronized sound, is designed to summon the peculiar terror of a child watching a mother or father transform in surreal and some-times monstrous fashion under the influence of intoxicants.

For critics Celeste Watkins-Hayes, Rikki Byrd and Candice Merritt, the stark distinctions between Teresa and Paula are less evident when the women are situated within the socio-political context of what they call 'the sexualized drug economy, one in which a health crisis was framed as a "crisis of criminality"'. They view Paula and Teresa as 'symbiotic actors within this punishing economic structure' (2019: 82). Indeed, while Teresa may assume the role of surrogate mother in relation to Chiron, she is also implicated in his misfortune as the romantic partner of a dealer, whose income presumably, at least in part, finances the running of the home in which Chiron seeks refuge. Additionally, Watkins-Hayes, Byrd and Merritt point out that Paula is not without agency or nuance. She does have a trajec-tory in the film, and although it is not the primary focus, her transformations are almost as profound as Chiron's. Paula moves from being a nurse and caring mother (see Figure 2.7) to a severely suffering addict, to a woman in recovery who wants to help others. This trajectory, for the authors, means that Paula 'demonstrates a complex femininity, one that does not allow us to affix easy stereotypes and controlling images on her' (86).

In the end, Jenkins does offer Paula redemption. The scene with Paula in the third section of the film goes a long way toward allowing the audi-ence to empathize with her, as she weeps and begs Chiron for forgiveness, or at least a tentative reconciliation. The scene is set in the 'Peachtree Drug Rehabilitation Centre' where Paula is in recovery, and she tells Chiron that she hopes to stay on and perhaps help others in similar circumstances. Both characters wear green and blue, returning them to the positive colour sche-matics of the first section of the film. Paula, tearfully, struggles to light

Figure 2.7 Paula cares for Chiron as a child, caressing his head.

a cigarette and tells Chiron that, although she mistreated him, she never stopped loving him. This scene is deeply emotional and Jenkins notes that the cast and crew 'cried every damn take' (quoted in Whipp 2016). In an extraordinary reading of this moment, Rizvana Bradley argues that this confession is 'the affective catalyst for, and driving force behind, the film's enigmatic ending' (2017: 51). Paula's admission of both love and failure influences Chiron's decision to visit Kevin and to make his own admission of loneliness and loss. Referencing the history of 'racial slavery's gendered social afterlife', Bradley argues that, 'Paula's revelation of her unwavering love for her son exposes a fundamental secret of black motherhood: that the practice of restrained filial intimacy is fundamentally entangled with love and loss' (ibid.). Paula insists on her love for Chiron, a love that has endured even this crippling addiction, while acknowledging the toll this addiction has taken on her child. Ultimately, as Bradley summarizes, for Paula, 'love is and perhaps can only ever be that which survives' (52).

Conclusion: Undoing stereotype

This chapter has provided an overview of cinematic depictions and stereotypes of Black masculinity from the 1970s onward, focusing on Blaxploitation and New Black Realism and their relevance to *Moonlight*. Yet, while stereotypes are undoubtedly reductive and damaging, they are also remarkably enduring and get reworked, undone and redone across time. This may be because, as Ruth Amossy argues, the stereotype allows for recognition and familiarity of the text on the part of the reader or viewer while also being 'a common place in which emotional identification can occur' (1982: 37). Jenkins references a familiar history of Black representation in Hollywood, but he gently strips stereotypes of their potency, revealing them to be false or incomplete. Jenkins discloses the nature of masculinity as performance by returning at key moments to Chiron's interior life, a focus that is also brought to bear on another significant aspect of his identity, his sexuality, which will be discussed in the following chapter.

3 *Moonlight* as Queer Cinema

As James Baldwin writes, 'The sexual question and the racial question have always been entwined' (Baldwin 2014: 64). One of the most significant ways in which *Moonlight* counters dominant representations of Black masculinity is through its presentation of a Black gay man. *Moonlight* has achieved great commercial and mainstream success within an industry that, when it tells queer love stories, has tended to prioritize white, middle-class LGBT narratives. Many critics lauded the film's pioneering depiction of queer sexualities in minority communities and the sensitive portrayal of the difficulties of a gay adolescence (Als 2016; Copeland 2017; Bastién 2017). The film's focus on the intersectionality of Chiron's identity also serves to highlight histories of the audio-visual representation of Black queer people. In this chapter, I consider the film's position among LGBTQ-themed films of the 2000s and 2010s and then outline a brief history of Black queer films, filmmakers and critical debates. I then turn to the question of whether *Moonlight* is more fittingly categorized as queer or LGBT cinema by focusing on debates around gender, intimacy, the film's elision of sex and the ending.

Situating *Moonlight*: Queer and/or LGBT filmmaking

Moonlight's Oscar win for Best Picture was heralded as a groundbreaking achievement for the LGBT community. GLAAD President and CEO Sarah Kate Ellis tweeted that the win 'sends a strong message to the film industry that it needs to embrace inclusive stories if it wants to remain competitive and relevant' (quoted in Townsend 2017). Although films such as Ang Lee's *Brokeback Mountain* (2005), Todd Haynes's *Carol* (2015) and Kimberly Peirce's *Boys Don't Cry* (1999) had been nominated and won Oscars in the past, *Moonlight* was the first to scoop the Best Picture award. Indeed, the film's publicity posters in the wake of its win proclaimed, 'it changes everything'. In the *Guardian*, Guy Lodge acknowledges that the film, although

DOI: 10.4324/9780429055294-3

not radical, is nonetheless a 'pathbreaker' in the history of LGBT cinema (2017a). Lodge's statement points to a tension between *Moonlight*'s status as mainstream and innovatory, and this difficulty in categorizing the film speaks to wider debates about universality and specificity in queer and LGBT cinema more broadly.

Definitions of queer cinema have been offered by many different critics and filmmakers. Benshoff and Griffin take, perhaps, the widest view of queer cinema in their definition, and they include potential markers such as films made by queer filmmakers; featuring queer actors, themes and characters; reception and reception practices; a 'gay' or 'camp' aesthetic; and the re-examination of old classics to look for repressed or hidden LGBT elements (2004: 2). They include both avant-garde and underground filmmaking as well as mainstream and commercial works. Queer film study, they argue, involves an understanding of sexualities on screen 'as complex, multiple, overlapping, and historically nuanced, rather than immutably fixed' (ibid.). However, for New Queer Cinema director Todd Haynes, queerness in film is about form and structure more than content. He notes that, while many define a 'gay' film by its characters, 'heterosexuality to me is a structure as much as it is a content' (in Wyatt 1993: 8). Such a reading accords with the formal innovations of the New Queer Cinema movement of the 1980s and 1990s, whose 'fragmented subjectivities' and 'dystopic' themes served as artistic responses to the horrors and losses of the AIDS crisis (Arroyo 1993: 90).

New Queer Cinema was, for the most part, an arthouse movement, grounded in film festivals and auteur aesthetics (Rich 2004: 16). Mainstream Hollywood also responded to shifting social attitudes around homosexuality and queer identities in the 1990s and particularly the 2000s. The most significant film of this period is Lee's *Brokeback Mountain*, an expansive and emotional tale of love in the closet, set among cowboys in Wyoming in the 1960s and 1970s. The film, starring Heath Ledger and Jake Gyllenhaal as the central couple, was nominated for nine Academy Awards and won five. Many critics cited the film's gay plot but came to understand it really as a 'universal' story, with the following typical reaction: 'the fact that the love story involves two men is secondary because the movie's underlying theme is so universal' (quoted in Cooper and Pease 2008: 257). For Gary Needham, *Brokeback Mountain* could be both indie and queer, popular and specific, where 'labelling it queer is a way of suggesting that it unsettles conventions, common sense assumptions and concepts of what is normal and normative' (2010: 2). By contrast, critic D.A. Miller slammed the film's 'universality' and mainstream appeal, citing its 'trim little, prim little craft', in which 'the Homosexual is not his sexuality, but his agonized attempt to fight it – touching proof of a certain devotion to normality after all' (2007: 50).

Brokeback Mountain brought to the fore issues of the universal and the particular that would continue through the 2010s. *Moonlight* is certainly part of a mainstreaming of LGBT cinema, including popular hits such as Lisa Cholodenko's *The Kids Are All Right* (2010), Abdellatif Kechiche's *Blue Is the Warmest Colour* (2013), Park Chan-wook's *The Handmaiden* (2016) and Luca Guadagnino's *Call Me By Your Name* (2017). These films share a merging of arthouse and mainstream filmmaking in terms of production companies, audiences and critical reception and the 'auteur' status of their directors. Of these films, both *The Kids Are All Right* and *Call Me By Your Name* provoked similar debates around the tension between universality and queer specificity in mainstream Hollywood film – debates that would also circle around *Moonlight*. In the case of *The Kids Are All Right*, critics praised the film not because of its depiction of a gay family but, rather, because the family was 'normal' (see Walters 2012: 924)

By 2017, when *Call Me By Your Name* was released, debates around universality in queer film had themselves gone mainstream. One of the major critiques of the film was the way that it ignores the AIDS crisis in favour of a nostalgic beauty designed to appeal to mainstream, i.e., straight, audiences. Indeed, director Guadagnino, himself gay, explicitly states that he wanted to create a 'powerful universality' achieved through beautiful landscapes and high art references and by excluding explicit sex scenes (quoted in Lee 2017a). Several critiques of *Call Me By Your Name* picked up on these issues of beauty, universality and the absence of explicit queer sex, and many included *Moonlight* in their analyses. Thus, for Billy Gray, writing in *Slate* about both films, 'the dignified aesthetics rob the films of their erotic potential' (2017).

For E. Alex Jung, the recent wave of commercially successful, Hollywood-endorsed films with LGBT themes and characters should be classed as LGBT cinema rather than queer film. Including *Call Me By Your Name* and *The Kids Are All Right* among their ranks, but not *Moonlight*, Jung characterizes these films in the following terms: 'They encapsulate a [...] catholic spirit: rather than assert difference, they point out similarities ... They're safe, often boring, and sentimental, following familiar emotional arcs to tell a "universal story"' (2018). Underlying these debates is the question of what constitutes a queer film as opposed to, or alongside, an LGBT-themed film. While New Queer Cinema was defined as a relation of margin to centre, indie to Hollywood, what happens when films with LGBT themes and characters are conceived, produced, or awarded by mainstream Hollywood? Michele Aaron aptly summarizes this conundrum, asking, 'how can a marriage between the popular and the radical be sustained when such an association erodes the very meaning of each?' (2004: 8).

Alexander Doty defines queer films as those that 'challenge or transgress established straight or gay and lesbian understandings of gender and sexuality' (1998: 149). A key term in this definition is the notion of 'established understandings', a sense in which both straight and queer normative definitions and ideas about sexuality change over time. Indeed, while the New Queer Cinema movement was lauded for its innovative and radical aesthetics, it was spearheaded and largely publicly embodied by white middle-class men. Indeed, as director Pratibha Parmar states,

> I am wary of talking about an overarching queer aesthetic, as my sensibility comes as much from my culture and race as from my queerness. In queer discourses generally there is a worrying tendency to create an essentialist, so-called authentic queer gaze.
>
> (1993: 175)

One might, therefore, argue that the persistent association of whiteness with LGBT film movements was a 'norm' or an 'established understanding' that women and minority filmmakers have sought to address and transgress. In the following sections, I attempt to address some of these debates around whether *Moonlight* can be considered a queer movie or one that is LGBT-themed. I examine the significance of race in relation to Chiron's sexuality in *Moonlight*, suggesting that a reading of the film through the lens of both race and sexuality, alongside queer critics of colour, produces a complex vision of the character's sexuality and the queerness of the film.

Moonlight: Black and queer in film and theory

Sex and sexuality are fundamentally bound up in questions of racial and ethnic identity. Both are concepts of the body and the body as it is lived by particular individuals in a specific social world in relation to dominant norms: whiteness and heterosexuality. Throughout the 1990s and 2000s, mainstream Hollywood continued to focus principally on the figure of the white, cisgender and middle-class protagonist. Scholars such as Judith Halberstam (2000) and Jennifer Devere Brody (2007) have pointed out the ways in which racial and ethnic minorities are not only marginalized in queer stories but actively erased by 'history's white lies', specifically in the film *Boys Don't Cry*. In relation to *The Kids Are All Right* and its presentation of the upper-middle class, white LGBT family, Tammie M. Kennedy writes that 'gaining acceptance [...] into the heteronormative society often depends on 'squelch[ing] racial, ethnic, socioeconomic, and gender diversity' (2014: 119).

Within this context, *Moonlight* was hailed as the first film to shatter the 'lavender ceiling' (O'Hara 2017), but it is far from the first film about queer Black lives. As L.H. Stallings reminds us, in response to a review that cited the 'groundbreaking' nature of the kissing scene, 'there have been Black gay men kissing on film in Black gay films' (2019: 343). Recent films like Dee Rees's *Pariah* (2011) and Sean Baker's *Tangerine* (2015) and television shows such as Ryan Murphy's *Pose* (2018–present, FX Network) and Justin Simeon's *Dear White People* (2017–2021, Netflix) all engage with Black queer sexualities in their characterization and themes. Moreover, it is particularly important to recognize *Moonlight*'s antecedents within the New Queer Cinema movement. In the late 1980s and 1990s, Marlon Riggs's *Tongues Untied* (1989), Isaac Julien's *Looking for Langston* (1989), Jennie Livingston's *Paris is Burning* (1990) and Cheryl Dunye's *The Watermelon Woman* (1996) all offered important depictions of the Black queer community. Each of these films employed the kind of formal innovations that came to be associated with the New Queer Cinema movement: they mixed narrative and documentary, history and fiction, by melding personal reflections with fictional plots or abstract sequences.

Of the films cited above, the documentary *Paris is Burning* has had the most enduring influence, and it is also the only one made by a white director. Charting the lives of Black and Hispanic queer people in New York's ball scene in the late 1980s and 1990s, the film presents a unique vision of the drag scene in New York and particularly the lives of trans women. For Daniel T. Contreras, *Paris is Burning* occupies an unusual position in the history of race and queer cinema, as 'one of the very few New Queer Cinema films that directly and complexly dealt with race at all in an unavoidably queer context' (2004: 120). However, the film is also critiqued for its 'white ethnographic gaze' by hooks, who argues that 'outsider' Livingston's presentation of the ball scene as spectacle disconnects the viewer from the material hardships and violent discrimination experienced by the characters (2015: 149–51).

Tongues Untied by filmmaker, scholar and poet Marlon Riggs, offers perhaps the most sustained reflection on the lived experience of Black gay men and a call for recognition of the interconnectedness of Black and queer experience. Riggs's film melds personal testimony, archive footage and a poetic voiceover to outline the ways in which his sexuality marginalized him within the Black community, while his race made him feel like an outsider within the gay community. Ultimately, as Louise Wallenberg suggests, the film rejects these dualistic oppositions between identities and, instead, stresses 'that black queerness, or queer blackness, cannot be divided so as to serve or represent different communities at different times' (2004: 129). *Tongues Untied* ends with a call to brotherhood and love among Black gay men; as the voiceover states, 'Black men loving black men is the revolutionary act'.

A particularly potent form of homophobia cannot be ascribed to the Black community, and such assignations can be read as part of an enduring Othering on the part of white society and white racist oppression (Jones 2019; Simmons 1991; Johnson 2003). At the same time, as Patricia Hill Collins notes, 'race complicates the closeting process and resistance to it' (2005: 112). She summarizes the ways in which discourses of white homosexual visibility and images of Black hyper-heterosexuality impede the development of 'a comprehensive analysis of Black sexuality that speaks to the needs of straight and gay Black people alike' (106). Writing of film and media representation, Riggs notes the particular homophobia of what he calls the 'Black Pack', a group of Black male entertainers popular at the time of his writing in 1991. He condemns the ways in which figures such as Eddie Murphy and characters such as Blaine Edwards (Damon Wayans) and Antoine Merriweather (David Alan Grier) construct and then mock the figure of what he calls the 'Negro Faggot'. A weak and effeminate individual, they are ridiculed and scorned, used as a source of comedy and derision, having nothing at all to do with, as Riggs notes, the actual lived experience of Black gay men.

Riggs views the creation of this figure as the 'desperate need for an Other *within* the community [… ,] an Other on which the blame for the chronic identity crises afflicting the Black male psyche can be readily displaced' (1991: 390). This Other can, therefore, act as a receptacle for the fears and anger that living in a racist society generate; indeed, Riggs continues, noting that although these figures may incite laughter, 'the representation of Negro Faggotry disturbingly parallels and reinforces America's most entrenched racist constructions around African-American identity' (391). E. Patrick Johnson draws on Riggs's work, and he charts a course in the latter half of the twentieth century in which a notion of 'authentic' Blackness is consistently coupled to heterosexuality, with the resultant separation of homosexuality from Black identity. Johnson argues that Black gay men were consistently represented as, and ridiculed for, being effeminate. As he elucidates, 'the representation of effeminate homosexuality as disempowering is at the heart of the politics of hegemonic blackness [...] for to be ineffectual is the most damaging thing one can be in the fight against oppression' (2003: 220). Of course, within this schema, femininity is also branded as weakness, for it is the perceived feminine traits of the Black gay man that are ridiculed. Johnson cites hooks, who argues that 'much black male homophobia is rooted in the desire to eschew connection with all things deemed "feminine" and that would, of course, include black gay men' (227). In the following sections, I track the popular and academic reception of *Moonlight* and how it engages gender, sex and sensuality and intimacy and quiet to consider whether we can call *Moonlight* LGBT-themed, queer, or as Johnson argues, 'quare' (2019).

Viewing *Moonlight*

The reception of *Moonlight* among online journalists and bloggers in the LGBT community was, for the most part, extremely positive. Many online reviewers of the film, some Hispanic as well as Black, spoke of the profound connection they felt to *Moonlight*. Many evoked painful feelings of being 'in the closet' as children or adolescents within their own particular communities. Hilton Als, in a moving essay in the *New Yorker*, writes of his profound connection to the character of Chiron, through his Black and queer identities: 'did I ever imagine, during my anxious, closeted childhood, that I'd live long enough to see a movie like "Moonlight," Barry Jenkins's brilliant, achingly alive new work about black queerness?' (2016). Angelica Jade Bastién writes about her own 'highly emotional' response to the film, a response that was grounded in 'aspects of my life I have been trying to block out — my upbringing in Miami, my family's financial struggles, the stunning loneliness of growing up between two worlds as an Afro-Latina' (2017). Others saw their own memories reflected in Chiron's suffering: Michael Cuby describes his own anxiety at watching Little being chased through the streets: '[it] gave me vivid flashbacks [...] I could feel fear in my heart' (2017).

Many viewers also felt that *Moonlight* was firmly grounded in the desire for social and political progress and change, reflecting ideas of queer as a 'political allegiance [...] to social and cultural transformation' (Stacy and Street 2007: 1). For Bahamian filmmaker Sekiya Dorsett, *Moonlight* is 'written in history', because the lives and loves of 'black and brown queer individuals were seen' (quoted in O'Hara 2017). Steven W. Thrasher (2016) links *Moonlight* explicitly to Riggs's influential *Tongues Untied* and its focus on the transformative power of Black love. For activist Tiq Milan, *Moonlight* is deeply grounded in the social context in which it was released, one of horrific police brutality and an epidemic of murder against Black trans women. He notes that the Black queer community was 'looking for some gentleness. Some stillness', which they found, he writes, in *Moonlight* (quoted in O'Hara 2017).

Moonlight's reception among academics is less straightforwardly laudatory; notably, the heteronormative masculinity Chiron embodies as Black in the third section of the film is examined by a number of critics. Drawing on the work of Riggs, Stallings argues that *Moonlight* 'offers updates of hegemonic blackness' that 'maintain gender binaries in which the feminine and femininity continue to be violently devalued' (2019: 342). For Stallings, *Moonlight* 'critiques homophobia without actually addressing femme phobia' and the persistent devaluation of the feminine in Black men. This absence of the Black queer feminine haunts the film, whereby the only acceptable image of Black queer men, and perhaps Black masculinity more broadly, is one that disavows femininity (ibid.). Stallings also links Paula to an overall 'irresolution of the feminine and women' (349).

Rinaldo Walcott cites the evocation of stereotype as one of the more discomforting aspects of *Moonlight*. He suggests that the film is 'steeped' in stereotypes about Black queer men in particular and, pondering the film's reception, argues that 'viewers celebrate the film because these stereotypes do not fully come to fruition' (2019: 337). He mentions many of the characteristics that connect the film to New Black Realism, such as setting, characterization and the coming-of-age narrative, and cites critiques of the genre for its homophobia. He notes additionally that bullying has become 'one of the central tropes in all of contemporary queer cinema', a 'popular queer film normativity that mainstream audiences are now socialized to be comfortable with' (440). Certainly, there have been a number of films in the 2010s looking at queer teen sexualities that feature bullying or exclusion, such as Desiree Akhaven's *The Miseducation of Cameron Post* (2018), *Pariah* and David Freyne's *Dating Amber* (2020).

Walcott further argues that *Moonlight* trades on stereotypes of Blackness in order to disrupt them, and one of these stereotypes is an imagined lack of intimacy between Black men. In this sense, he finds the ending 'deeply dissatisfying' in its refusal to offer a 'credible sex scene' (2019: 340). Stallings also cites the lack of sexual intimacy between Kevin and Chiron as a feature of the film's refusal to engage with femininity and Black queerness: 'kissing was represented as adolescent sexual exploration, but in the greater narrative of Black masculinity (in the film), grown Black men do not kiss each other' (2019: 350). La Marr Jurelle Bruce, although later revising his opinion somewhat, describes his initial disappointment with the ending of the film, wishing for 'a fourth act with Black being touched, held, clutched, embraced, caressed, stroked, kneaded, and needed' (2019: 356). Bruce's desire for happy romantic resolution is echoed by Trevante Rhodes, who imagines Chiron and Kevin, '90 years old […] now walking hand in hand in the park' (quoted in Brathwaite 2017).

There have been many debates about the representation of sex and intimacy in relation to mainstream LGBT-themed films. Mainstream films depicting same-sex female relationships have been widely critiqued for their explicit, even pornographic, depiction of sex designed to appeal to the male gaze. Notable examples include *The Handmaiden* and *Blue Is the Warmest Colour*. By contrast, popular films featuring gay male protagonists often cut away from, elide, or skim over the explicit representation of sex. Referring to the commercial and critical success of *Moonlight*, as well as films like *Brokeback Mountain*, Guy Lodge in the *Guardian* asks: 'does *Moonlight* show that gay cinema has to be sexless to succeed?' (2017b).

Call Me By Your Name was also subject to critique for its refusal to represent explicit gay sex and a concomitant kowtowing to the tastes and sensibilities of a 'universal', i.e. straight audience. For Guadagnino, the decision to pan away from Elio and Oliver's first sexual encounter maintains their privacy and avoids 'a sort of unkind intrusion' (quoted in Miller 2018). Miller was far from convinced by such an assertion. Instead, he links the refusal to show gay sex to the film's 'beautification campaign', where all that is ugly, including gay sex and what he calls the 'unlovely spectacle of blood, shit, and pain', must be expelled from the visual field (ibid.).

By contrast, David Greven suggests that the distance and delicacy employed by *Call Me By Your Name* in relation to sex is at one with the film's themes of 'longing to the point of deprivation' (2018). He summarizes: 'rather than some kind of disciplinary refusal to allow us the pleasure of same-sex sex, the decision to cut away here is an artistic choice meant to convey a larger thematic' (ibid.). Greven's words are instructive when we consider *Moonlight*'s elision of overt sexual exchanges. Might the choice to close the film at a moment of emotional, physical but not sexual touch speak to the wider aesthetic and emotional patterns in the film? In the rest of this chapter, I discuss the issue of gender in *Moonlight*, as well as images of quiet and consider how some critics have framed the film's choice of intimacy over sex differently, placing it within the context of Black, queer and working-class sexuality.

Moonlight: Gender, quiet and quare

Although *Moonlight* does not offer an image of a Black queerness that overtly embraces femininity, the film uses symbolism to associate Chiron with the feminine, such as the images of water, mirrors and moonlight (Berger 1973). These feminine symbols are not devalued but, rather, presented as moments when something essential about Chiron is revealed to the audience. Indeed, Taylor Barfield links Chiron through water to the gods and a mythological feminine, specifically the Yoruban goddess, Yemoja (2017). Yemoja has also been associated with queer theory and with queer Black authors such as Audre Lorde because the goddess embodies a fluid sexuality: 'she has the power to shift, change, and display an ambiguous sexuality' (Otero and Falola 2013: xxi). Moreover, although we see an image of a hegemonic, physically powerful and emotionally restrained masculinity, the film also looks beneath the surface and reveals this image to be a façade.

Indeed, in the film's presentation of a gender performance that can be assumed and altered depending on context, Chiron's final display of hegemonic masculinity can be aligned with Mary Anne Doane's seminal reading of femininity, in which she notes that 'womanliness is a mask which can be worn or removed' (Doane 1999: 427). Thus, when Black meets Kevin in the diner, Kevin expresses surprise at his appearance, noting his bulk. We also see Chiron remove the gold fronts on his teeth in order to eat his meal, and later Kevin teases him about these embellishments, asking, 'why you got them damn fronts?'. The fronts are a mask of masculinity to be 'worn or removed', and this reading is underscored by the song that plays as they get into Chiron's car after the diner scene, Jidenna's 'Classic Man' (2015). The opening lines of this song refer to the performance of a certain kind of masculinity, one that deceives women about the singer's true nature: 'I can pull the wool while I'm being polite [...] I can be a bull while I'm being polite'. The 'Classic Man' is polite to women, while a 'bull' lurks underneath, a deception that, in a sense, is the opposite to Chiron, who appears tough and hulking on the outside but with a hidden gentleness underneath. For Doane, the woman who took on the man's world 'felt compelled to compensate for this theft of masculinity by over-doing the gestures of feminine flirtation' (1999: 427). In a similar sense, Chiron exaggerates the gestures of masculine toughness in his exterior presentation – fronts, muscles, car, guns – in order to counteract his queer interior.

For Zaman, 'Jenkins imbues Chiron with a palpable queerness' (2016: 42), and part of this queerness, I argue, comes from Chiron's hesitant watchfulness throughout the film. In fact, Jenkins chose the actors because of their eyes, their look and gaze, and, therefore, this feature is of prime importance to our understanding of Chiron's character (Coyle 2016). Chiron's gaze is not one of mastery and control that sees and seeks to understand and dominate but, rather, a furtive vigilance. It recalls Richard Dyer's distinction between masculine looking and feminine watching in visual media in which women's looks are of a vigilant surveillance: 'women do not so much look at men as watch them' (1982: 63), a watchfulness born of threats to bodily safety. In terms of visual representation, Dyer argues that, while the female model retains a constant awareness of the presence of a viewer, the male model's look suggests 'an interest in something the viewer cannot see – it certainly does not suggest any interest in the viewer' (ibid.).

If we consider the regimes of looking in *Moonlight*, it is evident that Chiron's patterns of watchfulness connect him to a feminized hesitancy rather than a masculine dominance or indifference. In the presence of others, his habit of looking out from beneath his eyebrows, of glancing and then turning away and of surveying a scene from a distance all align him with a cautious gaze (see Figure 3.1). As John Berger writes of this self-surveillance, a woman 'has to survey everything she is and everything she does because how she appears to others, and ultimately how she appears to men,

Figure 3.1 Chiron's cautious and watchful gaze.

is of crucial importance for what is normally thought of as the success of her life' (1973: 46). Chiron must be watchful, for others have seen something in him, connected to his sexuality, and viewed it as weakness, as something to be exploited or abused. Indeed, far from conveying an indifference to the viewer, Chiron demonstrates a painful awareness of how others' perceptions of him can impact and endanger him. From the moment when he first meets Juan and the older man takes him to a cafe to the final moments of the film when he eats with Kevin, Chiron constantly visually assesses the world around him. This sense of surveillance is also captured in the 360-degree shots that punctuate the film. Such need for care is underscored by Juan, who tells the boy not to sit with his back to the door, so that people can't catch you by surprise. Indeed, in the cafe scene with Kevin, Chiron sits with his gaze carefully trained alternately on his friend and on the cafe door.

One particular scene with Kevin also highlights a queering of gender and forms of looking. After Kevin and Chiron speak for the first time as adults, the film moves into an abstract, poetic dream sequence depicting Kevin smoking outside of the cafe where he works. A track from the film's original score plays in the background, with its tremulous violin, and we see a medium shot and a close up of Kevin under the stark and radiant yellow light of the cafe. As the shot moves into close up, smoke tumbles lazily, effortlessly, out of Kevin's mouth, as he looks directly at the camera with a coy, curious, inviting gaze (see Figure 3.2). This scene reminded me of other moments in film, particularly those in which women have looked directly at the camera. In Hitchcock's *Vertigo* (1958), for example, this moment becomes a way for the audience to identify directly with the character of Judy rather than Scottie. It is a moment that breaks the male-dominated identification of the previous sections of the film and lets the viewer in on

Figure 3.2 Kevin looks directly at the camera.

a secret that the central male character does not know. In a similar sense, Kevin's flirtatious and knowing glance in this scene might suggest that he knows more about his own queerness, and that of Chiron, than has been represented in the dialogue.

Chiron's watchfulness can also be connected to his quietness. Even at some of the most painful and exceptional moments of his life, such as when Juan admits that he deals drugs to Paula, Chiron remains silent. Kevin even recognizes Chiron, in part, because of his reticent nature: 'still can't say more than three words at a time, huh?'. Jung, who heartily laments the bland mainstreaming of queer film, regards Chiron's quietness as part of the film's queerness, noting that 'it's in the liminality of *Moonlight,* where what often resonates are the things left unsaid' (2018). Indeed, much of what is left unsaid in *Moonlight* relates to Chiron's sexuality. This 'unsaid' plays out mainly through his relationship with Kevin, but there are other moments: the pause at the end of his childhood tussle with Kevin, his dance in front of the mirror in school, his silence in the face of the guidance counsellor who calls him a 'boy' and the subtly flirtatious interaction between Chiron and the dealer who works for him in the opening part of the third section when they both tease each other for not having girlfriends. This quietness and watchfulness, the unsaid of sexuality, again recalls for some viewers their own experiences of childhood and adolescence. Josh Lee writes that *Moonlight* connects with his own adolescent fears and desire for safety, noting that many queer kids 'were forced to swap the naiveté of "normal" childhood for constant awareness of our surroundings and any potential threats' (2017).

Furthermore, Kevin Quashie discusses depictions of Black 'quiet', suggesting that Blackness in the public imagination is associated with loud, public and expressive resistance. He argues for representations of quietude and Blackness that 'gesture away from caricatures [...] that are either racist or intended to counter racism' and instead 'suggest what is essentially and indescribably human' (2012: 334). Quiet, then, can be just as powerful and expressive as speech, as something 'inevitable, essential, sovereign; expressive and lush' (10). For Jenkins, who admits he is not very loquacious himself, memories come not as words but as 'feelings and moments' (quoted in McDonald 2016). He believes that silence allows for a truer glimpse of character and that 'when people are in repose, you really see beneath the surface' (quoted in Rapold 2016). Quiet in the film is linked to a powerful intimacy between Kevin and Chiron, an intimacy that eschews overt illustration of sexual activity.

Critics suggest that images of Black intimacy and romance have been largely absent from Hollywood film from Blaxploitation to the 1990s (Guerrero 1993: 144; Collier 1989). Riggs argues that images of Black male sexuality swing between two distorted poles: an arrested hyposexuality and an out-of-control hypersexuality (1991: 392). Jacquie Jones adds that, as Hollywood films became increasingly violent, sexual intimacy was inscribed 'as the only legitimate humanizing contact' (1993: 248). At the same time, Black men in film were sexually 'on display', and 'depicted as overly developed and animal forms' (ibid.). Thus, just as Quashie links quiet to forms of humanization, Jones argues that the absence of images of Black male intimacy mean that 'the audience is never able to conceive of the Black male character as completely human, even beyond the temporal film reality' (250). Intimacy, here, is connected to humanization both on and off screen, just as quiet evokes something redolently human for Quashie as well. Some queer Black viewers appreciated this focus on intimacy rather than sex, with one, Matthew Progress, writing, 'I've never seen a feature film capture love between black men in such a holistic way' (quoted in Parris 2016).

The gay romance depicted in *Moonlight* primarily relies on a tender emotionality and a soft and gentle eroticism. In the only scene that explicitly depicts sexual activity, Kevin manually stimulates Chiron to orgasm on a beach. The beach scene as a whole resonates with quiet and what is left unsaid. Given that critics point to the beauty of *Moonlight* (as well as *Call Me By Your Name*) as a feature that universalizes the film and detracts from its queerness, it is worth noting that the visual splendour of other scenes is muted at the beach and in the diner. While much of the second section of the film is shot under fluorescent light, the boys sit on the beach at night. The light carries only shades of grey differentiating sea and sand, and the only bright colour in the scene is the yellow winking dots of light in the distance. Shot mostly in a reverse shot as the boys talk, the scene, nonetheless, captures moments of near silence, the breeze flowing in the background, such

Figure 3.3 An overhead two shot of Chiron and Kevin at the beach.

as when they look upward at the sky, captured in an overhead two shot (see Figure 3.3). The dialogue itself resonates with unspoken queries, wonderings and desires. Chiron asks, 'what kinda dude goes around giving another dude nicknames' (perhaps one who fancies you). When Kevin expresses surprise at how easily Chiron puffs on the joint, a brief mention of Paula and drugs in the house is all that is needed for Kevin to understand. There are gaps in their conversation, but they also reference silence explicitly, noting that when the ocean breeze blows through their neighbourhood, 'everything just get quiet', to which Chiron responds, 'and it's like all you can hear is your own heartbeat'.

Their moment of sexual intimacy is conducted in almost complete silence, particularly the lingering gaze they share before they kiss, again replete with the danger of an unspoken and perhaps unspeakable desire. Kevin moves quickly to unbuckle Chiron's belt, and the silence and speed of the masturbation does seem to speak to a covert and shadowy act. Walcott finds this scene somewhat stereotypical, noting that it is 'a certain kind of Black queer coming of age that many queer men will recall' (2019: 340). However, read within the film's schematic privileging of stillness, moonlight and the ocean, this moment is imbued with immense and intimate significance. Kevin does not shame or reject Chiron in its wake, and the camera lingers on the moment of their parting, and their hands touch gently as Chiron leaves his friend's car.

Moreover, other sensory apperceptions take the place of sight. There is no music in the scene, and instead, the quiet breeze thrums in the background, a breeze one can imagine glancing over the boys' faces. The sense of smell is also evoked in the scene: the thick plumes of the joint they smoke, the salty air from the sea and the smell of semen after Chiron ejaculates. The image of a hand grazing the sand, and the contact that accompanies Chiron's shudders, invites viewers to use the sense of touch as a mode of understanding and more importantly, feeling, the images. Laura Marks defines a mode of understanding film through senses other than sight as 'haptic' viewing in which the sense of touch is privileged over the sense of sight. Haptic images can be blurred, grainy, difficult to see. They are images of intimacy, ones that disorient the viewer, who 'suspends judgement [...] and tests the images by bringing them close' (Marks 2000: 181).

Yancy's introduction to a special journal edition on *Moonlight* takes intimacy as its central theme. Indeed, just as Marks highlights in relation to the haptic, Yancy admits that he was discombobulated by the 'touch' of the film: 'for me, *Moonlight*'s touch was disorienting [...] To say I "watched" *Moonlight* is probably inaccurate, especially as "watched" implies a species of [...] surveillance [...] I lost my bearings' (2019: 65). Within this context, both touch and orientation are key concepts. *Moonlight* depicts Chiron's orientation and disorientation in the world, and as a film about queer touch that is emotionally touching, it can unsettle, perhaps particularly in the way that it invites viewers to revisit their own childhoods. Or, as in Yancy's case, inviting him to think about how being 'a cisgender, heterosexual Black male is to be part and parcel of a world' (ibid.). In so far as the touch of the film can disorient, it is queer, where queerness, according to Anat Pick, involves a 'making strange' of the self in the world (2004: 105). Indeed, Sara Ahmed describes queerness as a kind of 'disorientation device', 'allowing the oblique to open up another angle on the world' (2006: 172). Indeed, E. Patrick Johnson's theorization of race, sexuality and class opens up another 'angle' on *Moonlight*, one that both orients and disorients a strictly 'LGBT-themed' reading of the film.

Baldwin references the primacy of race over sexuality when it comes to an individual's separation or incorporation into mainstream society. Responding to an interviewer's suggestion that both Black people and white gay people feel separated from conventional culture, Baldwin states:

> The sexual question comes after the question of colour; it's simply one more aspect of the danger in which all black people live. I think white gay people feel cheated because they were born, in principle, into a society in which they were supposed to be safe.
>
> (2014: 67)

Baldwin goes on to state that the 'unexpected' danger that white queer people are subject to is accompanied by 'the sense of feeling cheated of the advantages which accrue to white people in a white society' (ibid.). This is something that Black gay people do not experience, as their race already precludes them from a sense of entitlement to what Baldwin refers to as 'the American fantasies', the American Dream and attendant notions of equality and meritocracy (68). Baldwin goes on to note that 'the gay world as such is no more prepared to accept black people than anywhere else in society' (67).

Writing about the intersection of race, sexuality and class, E. Patrick Johnson begins with a quote from Baldwin: 'nobody *knows* my name' (2001: 2). The work goes on to register Johnson's unease with being named and interpellated as 'queer'. He outlines the limits on the uses of 'queer' in some critical theory, noting that in its undoing of binaries and its questioning of fixed identities, 'queer' 'is not necessarily embraced by gay, bisexuals, lesbians, and transgendered people of color' (4). Citing critic John Champagne's work on *Tongues Untied*, he notes that Champagne refuses to acknowledge the importance of experience as evidence – that is, that Riggs's personal experiences of racism and homophobia count in the interpretation of his work. Champagne elides the significance of race and class to individual experience, viewing 'bodily experience as anti-intellectual' (7). Johnson, thus, suggests that the tendency of white queer critics to ignore the fact that 'white bodies are discursively and corporeally naturalized as universal' means that bodily experiences, specific to Black people, remain uninterrogated (ibid.).

Johnson proposes the word 'quare' as an alternative to queer, whereby class and racial identities are not subsumed into the broader category of 'queer'. Having grown up in Ireland and been schooled in convents, I had heard the word quare long before I heard the word queer. Therefore, I am tickled by Johnson's use of the term, and he references quare's Irish ancestry, as meaning both 'odd' and 'strange' as well as, at least in one text, homosexuality. For Johnson, quare studies is defined as 'a theory of sexuality that accounts for its relationality to other embodied ways of knowing, particularly in terms of race and class' (2019: 71). Blackness cannot be subsumed into queerness, and emotions and bodily experience have to be included as valid and validating categories and methods of analysis, leading to a 'meatier politics of resistance' (Johnson 2001: 10). Ultimately, the failure to ground discourse in materiality and lived social experience 'is to privilege the position of those whose subjectivity, outside the realm of gender and sexuality, have never been subjugated' (12), that is, economically privileged cisgendered white people.

Tellingly, Johnson views *Moonlight* as quare. *Moonlight*, he argues, opens a space in which gender and sexuality can be explored *alongside* race and class. He notes that masculinity in *Moonlight* is neither hegemonic nor anti-hegemonic but, rather, what he terms a '*makeshift masculinity*', which is 'created from the scraps of one's life and grounded in a working-class epistemology or queerness that does not privilege "outness" or visibility' (2019: 71). He argues that poverty can create material conditions that necessitate a different relationship to gender and sexuality than what is understood by 'hegemonic queerness' (2019: 71). In thinking of *Moonlight* as quare, the scene of Kevin and Chiron's reunion stands as one of the most significant moments of the film. It is shot in real time over 20 minutes, a significant change of temporal pace for a film that has glossed and glanced over months, years and even decades in previous sections. Although the third section is, in fact, the one that Jenkins added to McCraney's play, the scene in the diner nonetheless has a theatrical feel, due to its real-time nature and how it is framed. It is shot almost as an enclosed world, a space and time sealed off from the outside – an impression that is enhanced by close up shots of the bell on the door, which signals entry and exit into the space of the diner. The diner itself feels both timeless and stuck in time – decorated in browns and reds, with leather booths, gumball machines, a juke box and short prim curtains on the windows, it recalls coming-of-age movies such as *Grease* (Kleiser 1978) and *American Graffiti* (Lucas 1973).

Diners are spaces in movies in which boys and girls meet and flirt, and this association carries through the sexual tension and excitement Chiron and Kevin evidently feel in their reunion. Significantly, Kevin tells Chiron to sit, and he will cook for him. Food was the first way Juan showed his interest and affection for Chiron as a child, by feeding him, first in a diner and then in his home. Within the context of poverty, food is of huge material significance: in 2019, 10.7 million children in the US lived with food insecurity, with this figure rising to 17 million in 2020 (Strochlic 2020). Although neither Kevin nor Chiron as adults appear to be living in food poverty, and Kevin even notes that Chiron does not look like he's been missing meals, the preparation of this meal connects them to a childhood in which, perhaps for both, food was not readily and easily available. The camera lingers in soft focus on Kevin's loving preparation of this meal of chicken breasts, rice, black beans, onions and peppers topped with fresh green herbs, a preparation that Johnson calls a 'mating ritual' (2019: 78) (see Figure 3.4).

This meal again connects Kevin to Juan, as two men who care for Chiron, and as Johnson notes, this is 'the foodstuff of the working poor and of the Afro-Caribbean' (2019: 78). Food is also one of the primary ways in which families, friends and caregivers share and show love: Kevin even references these associations of food with care, love and family, saying that this is 'grandma's rules, you know the drill, your ass eat, your ass speak'. As Gay Poole notes, 'the preparation of food requires thought, labour, time, and in some cases love, it is an ideal conduit for emotional language. It is possible to "say" things with food' (1999: 3). Megan Wilson offers a fascinating

Figure 3.4 The meal that Kevin cooks for Chiron.

reading of food and queer kinship in *Moonlight*. She notes the ways in which food is interlaced with the transformations in Chiron's life, in which his 'subjectivity and character development as a gay man is influenced by the nourishment he receives (or does not receive) from other people' (2019: 22). Chiron also breaks his self-imposed rules with Kevin: just as he persuaded Chiron to share a joint on the beach, Kevin offers him a small glass of wine, which Chiron gulps down as if it were water. In this way, food and wine proposed by Kevin provide Chiron with an access to physical pleasure and sensuality. The sharing of a meal with Kevin becomes part of Chiron's emotional journey and acts as precursor to the romantic intimacy they share in the closing sequence when they embrace.

Just as the beach scene resonates with what is left unspoken, so too does the scene in the diner rely on 'silence and knowing glances', in which 'so much is said in what isn't said' (Johnson 2019: 78). Kevin begins, for example, 'the last time we saw each other …' and stops, and although this seems to refer to Chiron being taken away in a police car, the viewer's mind immediately wanders to both the beach and the subsequent beating. Music is also used in this scene to fill in the gaps of what remains, thus far, unspoken between the two men. We find out that Barbara Lewis's 'Hello Stranger' (1963), a song about reconnecting with a lost love, is the track that brought Chiron into Kevin's mind. Lyrics like 'please don't tease me / like you did before / because I still love you so' render the implicit erotic charge between the two men explicit, allowing the music to speak in the place of dialogue. 'Hello Stranger' might also refer to how changed Kevin finds Chiron, or the stranger might also reference Chiron's estrangement or disorientation in relation to his queer self. In meeting Kevin, he is once again opening up and returning to a part of his self that has been suppressed since that night on the beach.

Johnson views the ending of the film as quare, in that it is 'off kilter', denying the viewer the satisfaction of sex and, instead, proposing 'something much more subtle, ambivalent, open ended' (2019: 79). Instead of offering the viewer closure, the film lingers, or to use Bruce's terminology, 'loiters' ambiguously (2019: 352). Chiron returns to Kevin's house, where Kevin boils water on the stove, and the image of a saucepan caught in a close up that invites us to remember the water Chiron boiled as a child for a solitary bath. The image of the lonely pot that recalls a lonely childhood frames the pivotal moment of this scene, in which Chiron declares, 'You're the only man who's ever touched me. The only one. I haven't really touched anyone, since'. Kevin has previously asked Chiron, 'who is you?', and yet, as the camera dwells on Kevin's face, he seems almost blindsided by the depth of Chiron's honesty. He recovers, and the penultimate image of the film (see Figure 3.5), a medium two shot of Chiron resting his head on Kevin's chest, echoes both the posture and dark, grainy lighting of the beach scene. It also mirrors the image and pose of Paula cradling Chiron's head as a child, connecting Kevin's embrace to a love experienced in childhood (see Figure 2.7). The men do not kiss but, instead, embrace with Kevin holding Chiron in silence and in stillness. Baldwin links the experience of touch to the overcoming of homophobia and fear, regarding corporeal, material experience as central to one's apprehension of the world: 'the capacity for experience is what burns out fear. Because the homophobia we are talking about is really a kind of fear […] It's really a terror of being able to be touched' (2014: 70). Gentle, wanted touch is an experience that soothes hate, and this overcoming of fear, combined with his silence throughout the rest of the film, makes Chiron's admission that he has never been touched since the night on the beach all the more powerful.

Figure 3.5 Chiron rests his head on Kevin's chest.

Conclusion

Jenkins, noting that Chiron has felt 'unworthy of love' for a very long time, talks about how Chiron's admission of how long he has lived without human contact 'takes a *lot*. It takes maybe 99 percent of him' (quoted in Brathwaite 2017). From a place of such brutal honestly, Jenkins says, 'you gotta build yourself back up' (ibid.). Therefore, this may be a moment not of ending but of beginning for Chiron. Indeed, the whole film has been about Chiron's journey, his transformations and the threads of similarity that carry over the first three decades of a life. As he notes, 'I built myself from the ground up'. In this sense, we might, ultimately, argue for the queerness, and quareness, of the film, as, according to Annamarie Jagose, 'queer is always already an identity under construction, a site of permanent becoming' (1997: 131). Kevin's embrace of Chiron, the supportive pose as he holds him to his chest, suggests that he will not have to undergo this transformation alone. Indeed, some of the first words that Kevin speaks to Chiron when Chiron enters the diner are 'I got you'. Although Kevin is talking about making dinner for his prodigal friend, these words are exactly those used by Juan in the swimming sequence. The shot at the end of the film, of the child Chiron in front of the waves, suggests that just as he learned to float and swim with Juan's help, perhaps he can learn to let go, and even to swim, with the tender support that intimacy with Kevin provides. In this sense, as Johnson memorably summarizes, 'intimacy might be the salve for the wound of poverty' (2019: 71).

4 Watching *Moonlight*

Narrative, setting and symbolism

This chapter examines how the particular aesthetic of *Moonlight* is created, examining its narrative structure, space, cinematography and music and colour symbolism. This chapter will first consider how *Moonlight* can be categorized in cinematic terms, particularly its position between arthouse and mainstream cinema. Next, the film's narrative structures will be examined, which combine the teleology of the coming-of-age narrative with less linear forms and that speak to the traditions of New Black Realism and what Diawara calls the 'Black expressive style' of storytelling in independent Black productions (1993: 13). The chapter then turns to the representation of the space of Liberty City in *Moonlight*, focusing on its relation to other 'hood' films and to ideas of beauty and realism. The final section will explore the symbolism and structuring of colour and music in *Moonlight*, combining attention to form and content.

What kind of film is *Moonlight*?

Moonlight was financed by the independent production company A24, whose history reflects *Moonlight*'s status as both within and just outside the mainstream. A24 was founded in 2012, and the name of the company apparently arises from the A24 road into Rome, where founder Danial Katz had the idea for the company (this road has arthouse connotations, as it is featured in a few Italian neo-realist works). Cited as a company that is 'disrupting Hollywood' (Baron 2017), A24 has been responsible for producing some of the most interesting coming-of-age dramas of recent years, such as Sofia Coppola's *The Bling Ring* (2013), Greta Gerwig's *Lady Bird* (2017) and Sean Baker's *The Florida Project* (2018). Directors and actors who have worked with A24 cite the control they have over their work, and they say that many of the stories told by A24 would not get to the big screen if not taken on by the company (Baron 2017). At the same time, A24's films

DOI: 10.4324/9780429055294-4

have been lauded by the Academy, garnering numerous nominations and awards at the Oscars. The company has also entered a deal with Apple TV+ to produce exclusive content for the streaming service, reportedly worth $1 billion (Lang 2018).

A24's status as between independent cinema and Hollywood reflects many of the debates around *Moonlight*, as well as Jenkins's own cinematic precursors. Jenkins notes that in film school, 'everyone was influenced by the same things: Steven Spielberg, James Cameron, Wes Anderson' (quoted in Pulver 2017). By contrast, he immersed himself in foreign film. Specifically, Jenkins has described himself as a 'superfan' of Denis, and he has stated that she is 'the world's greatest working filmmaker' (ibid.). Jenkins also mentions Lynne Ramsay who showed him that 'not all film directors were born with silver spoons in their mouths' (ibid.). He was also drawn to the work of Wong Kar-wai, whose love stories, *In the Mood for Love* (2000) and *Happy Together* (1997), recall the melancholy, sensitivity to emotion and rich colour schemes of *Moonlight*. Taiwanese auteur Hou Hsaio-hsien's *Three Times* (2005) also influenced the tripartite structure of *Moonlight*. Because of these influences, Jenkins has been called, somewhat sweepingly, 'the first major American Academy Award-winning director whose film lineage is distinctly non-American' (ibid.).

Moonlight also speaks to histories of African American filmmaking. Critics have highlighted the ways in which the film's aesthetics draw on this tradition, as well as how this artistic inheritance has been underexplored in the popular reception of the film. Racquel Gates notes that while many critics have been quick to draw connections between Jenkins and non-American, arthouse directors, the links between *Moonlight*'s aesthetics and those of African American precursors have been less studied. She names the example of *Belly* (1998), by Hype Williams (2017: 41), to which one might add Spike Lee's *Clockers* (1995), also mentioned in relation to style by *Moonlight* cinematographer James Laxton (in Kilday 2016). *Belly*'s colour palette of rich blues, striking visuals and its *film noir* feel recall the ways in which *Moonlight* uses colour to convey themes. Similarly, Dan Flory links the *noir* elements he locates in *Moonlight* to similar themes and aesthetics in the New Black Realist dramas of the 1990s (2009: 105–6). Gates cautions against a tendency to 'send the message that certain types of aesthetics can exist only in certain types of spaces', whereby *Moonlight* is moved from 'the industry's pejorative category, "black film"' to the more critically acceptable category of 'a film that happens to be black' (2017: 41).

Gates also notes that studies of Black cinema tend to focus on the politics of representation while neglecting aesthetics and style. This is what she calls a 'racialized politics of style' (2017: 40), along with the aesthetic of 'whiteness as beauty' that has dominated cinematic images. Colour film technology was designed to capture the colour palette of white skin, and 'racial bias has become an intrinsic part of the technologies of film and television, with a lasting impact on what makes it to the screen' (ibid.). Indeed, the technological history of cinematic lighting and filming is one that systematically rendered darker skin tones less visible and less realistic. 'Shirley Cards', a measuring device against which lab technicians developed colour photographs, were designed in the 1940s and 1950s, and featured a white, brown-haired woman, named 'Shirley' by Kodak executives (Caswell 2015). This meant that all skin tones were calibrated against the white standard of 'Shirley', meaning that darker skin appeared washed out, ashen, or difficult to discern. In the 1970s, change came from an unlikely source: furniture and chocolate companies, who complained that film could not capture nuances of shade and tone in their products (Roth 2009).

Black filmmakers, such as John Singleton and Spike Lee, learned to work with defective technologies and employed a number of 'tricks' to better illuminate their actors, such as moisturizing the actor's skin or lighting them more strongly. Recently, a new wave of cinematographers, mostly trained at Howard University, have been garnering praise for their illumination of Black skin on screen. Managing what Nadia Latif calls 'the built-in bias' of technology, cinematographers such as Laxton, Ava Berkofsky (*Insecure* 2016–present, HBO) and Bradford Young (*Pariah, 12 Years a Slave* and *Selma*) are transforming the way Black skin looks on screen. One technique they use relates to the colour palette of the film: 'drawing a rainbow of colours from the actors' skin itself to create something more vibrant and less concerned with being "real"' (Latif 2017). The spaces and faces of *Moonlight* and the rich blues, purples and pinks that saturate the visual field have certainly been praised widely in mainstream media for their beauty. Many of these discussions pair the film's beauty with another term, such as 'quiet beauty' (Shone 2016), 'misery and beauty' (Tate 2016) and 'aching beauty' (Nicholson 2016), thus linking the formal and the thematic. Yet these discussions, for Gates, can veer into fetishization, and she argues that such praise betrays the ways in which *Moonlight*'s images are 'beautiful precisely in the way that white images have traditionally been beautiful, and black ones have not' (2017: 44). Such beautification has habitually been equated with humanization – the ability of audiences to identify with and perceive the full humanity of the protagonists on screen, where 'the beautiful cinematography connotes that its characters are *worthy*' (40). *Moonlight*, she argues, risks bolstering 'established taste politics that [have] traditionally dictated an aesthetic marginalization and degradation for people of color' (44).

Gates's points are reinforced by a comment made by Laxton when describing how the neighbourhood of Liberty City was filmed. Reporter

Gregg Kilday describes the 'gritty' nature of the film's subject matter (an oft-evoked term in describing Black New Realist cinema), and Laxton notes that *Moonlight*'s visual style was a way to 'elevate' its content (quoted in Kilday 2016). In this sense, one might wonder what was 'low' in *Moonlight*'s themes that needed to be raised – an implicit assumption that beauty needs to be created *a priori* in such spaces. This is a view that Jenkins and McCraney do not share – they speak of a pre-existing beauty in Liberty City, one that they sought to capture rather than create. Heeding Racquel Gates's and Michael Boyce Gillespie's exhortation that the critic should focus on the aesthetics as well as the themes of Black cinema (2019), the following sections discuss narrative, space and cinematography, as well as colour and music in *Moonlight*.

Moonlight: Linear and cyclical narrative styles

In considering narrative in *Moonlight*, it is useful to turn to Diawara's identification of two distinct narrative modes in African American filmmaking of the 1990s: New Black Realism and the Black expressive style (1993: 3–25). As discussed in Chapter 2, linear narratives, such as those found in *Boyz N the Hood*, adopt a straightforward narrative arc with a clear beginning, middle and end and have concrete spatio-temporal parameters. The second narrative style Diawara identifies is the Black expressive style, incorporating 'cyclical' narration, irregular chronology and references to African traditions and myths (1993: 10). Diawara highlights the attributes that these films share with the jazz tradition as well as with the novels of Alice Walker and Toni Morrison. These films focus on 'the empowerment of Black people through mise-en-scène, and the rewriting of American history' (ibid.). The primary cinematic example Diawara draws on is Julie Dash's *Daughters of the Dust* (1991), which employs overlapping temporality in its exploration of the Gullah community on the island of St Helena in 1902. In line with Diawara's comment on the importance of mise-en-scène in cyclical narratives, the costumes that the women wear in the film are striking (flowing whites and creams, Edwardian lace gloves and bodices, loose-fitting bright white linen shift gowns) and they were cited by Beyoncé in her 2016 visual album, *Lemonade*.

  Moonlight reflects and was inspired by some of the narrative elements of New Black Realism's linear storytelling (Svetkey 2019), and the three-part structure of the story echoes the chronological structure of many coming-of-age narratives (Shary 2005). The film's triptych structure divides Chiron's life into 'I – Little', 'II- Chiron' and 'III – Black', clearly marking the passage of time. We witness Chiron grow and develop over a period of approximately 15–20 years, as he moves from boyhood into manhood, and the characters and settings both remain consistent and evolve around him. Juan, a major figure in Act I, is visually absent from the other sections of the film, while Terrel and Theresa appear only in Sections I and II. Paula and Kevin are present in Chiron's life across the three parts of the film, and this realist mode allows the viewer to witness the characters' evolution over time and in response to circumstances. Yet, beyond the three sections, the passage of time is not always clearly delineated. Indeed, McCraney's play, *In Moonlight Black Boys Look Blue*, has nonlinear plotting and narrative (Hans 2018). There are no intertitles that locate the action in space and time; instead, this knowledge is gleaned through dialogue or inferred through music and the ageing of the characters. For example, music by the rap group Goodie Mob plays in the car in Part III, suggesting both a time and a place: Atlanta in the mid-1990s. At the same time, Part III also features anachronistic diegetic music, Jidenna's 'Classic Man', a track that was released in 2016, although the scene itself is set in the 1990s.

Moreover, within each section, the period of time captured is uncertain. For example, in Section I, close analysis of Chiron's clothing reveals a sequence of approximately three connected moments – the initial meeting with Juan and Teresa, the day when he plays football and swims with Juan and the closing scenes in which Paula's drug addiction worsens, and Chiron discovers that Juan sells drugs to his mother. Yet, the action in this section could take place over weeks, months or even a year or two. This indeterminacy creates a sense not of time as repetition, habits and duration but, rather, time as a series of punctuated, significant moments that unfold like memories. Any film, of course, might be said to be made up of 'significant moments', but the difference in *Moonlight* is that the moments depicted are not necessarily remarkable events in and of themselves, but rather, they are important to Chiron.

In some instances, the full significance of these events is only divulged later in the film, often through repetition. Water is revealed as significant through the 'rhythmic and repetitious shots' characteristic of the Black expressive style (Diawara 1993: 10). Thus, the swimming scene with Juan is connected to intimacy with Kevin on the beach, which in turn refers to the solitary baths Chiron took as a child and his statement that he only drinks water as an adult. As a further example, the scene in which Chiron plunges his head into iced water, having been beaten by Kevin and the bullies, marks Chiron's transition from boy into man. This image reappears at the start of Section III of the film when the now-muscular Chiron bathes his head in water upon waking (see Figure 4.1). Shot from both beneath and behind his head, these are highly reminiscent of Lynne Ramsay's *We Need to Talk about Kevin* (2011), where they serve to connect Kevin to his mother Eva across space and time. In a similar sense, this immersion in water links

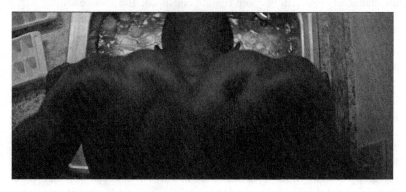

Figure 4.1 A muscular Chiron bathes his head in water upon waking.

Chiron across three stages of his life and creates capillaries that connect the teenager who was assaulted and the adult he has become.

Moonlight, thus, treats recognized rites of passage symbolically and through their emotional and private effects on the individual. Paula's worsening addiction is evoked by her shouting at Chiron, filmed through the prism of his child-like fear; his isolation is rendered in the solitary bath he takes; his gayness is hinted at through a scene in which he dances wholeheartedly in front of a mirror in school as some of his classmates look on sceptically. Chiron's arrest at the end of Part II is followed by a return to his child self at the start of Part III. In this privileging of emotion over progressive narrative action, *Moonlight* has been called a 'slow movie'. Citing a number of films that were released in 2016, Brooke Allen argues that. in contrast to the hectic speeds favoured by mainstream Hollywood, these films 'linger on the actor's visage', 'forego[ing] melodrama in favour of close attention to character and [finding] true drama in quiet, apparently mundane exchanges' (627). Indeed, although the actors are quite different in appearance, the three are united by facial expressions, gestures and habits that carry through the three chapters of the film. Chiron's tentative nervousness, his habit of lowering his head and glancing out from beneath his eyebrows and his use of water to self-soothe lend unity and circularity to the narrative structure of the film. This heightens the audience's affective and imaginative connection with the character, as we perceive his continuity across space and time not through realist physical resemblance but through emotion.

Finally, the ending of *Moonlight* further captures this tension between linear and cyclical narrative plotting. According to David Bordwell, the classical Hollywood film, 'ends with a decisive victory or defeat, a resolution of the problem and a clear achievement or non-achievement of the goals' (1985: 157). This statement both applies and does not apply to *Moonlight* and essentially rests on how one defines 'achievements' and 'goals'. At the end of the film, Chiron goes with Kevin to his home, and the film culminates with a two-shot of the pair, embracing on Kevin's couch. This ambiguous ending means that the viewer must infer, according, perhaps, to their own desires, whether Chiron and Kevin 'make it', and it is in line with the expressive Black filmmaking style and arthouse aesthetics. At the same time, Chiron's return to touch, affection and intimacy with Kevin, after many years of solitude and loneliness, can be read as a clear finale to the film's narrative journey. The ending does represent the attainment of a goal of sorts, within the film's own specific register, which is one that values emotional authenticity and intimate exchange.

The settings of *Moonlight*

The social and structural environment in which Chiron comes of age is Liberty City, Miami, Florida, and this urban space links the social world in which the protagonist comes of age to the New Black Realism of the 1990s and Blaxploitation films of the 1970s, which were also set in deprived urban areas. As such, *Moonlight* can be said to ground its story in a world that is familiar to movie-going audiences, one that might be considered a stereotype or at least a *leitmotif* of Black cinematic spatial representation. However, it is important to consider not only the 'what' that *Moonlight* represents but also the 'how' in terms of technique. *Moonlight* reworks the aesthetics of previous representations: Liberty City is rendered as beautiful under Jenkins and Laxton's lens, an aestheticization that is not without political portent.

The history of Liberty City as a 'black hyperghetto' (Jones 2019; Wacquant 2010) serves as a microcosm of the ways in which white government policies have systematically dislocated Black communities across the US in the twentieth century. Liberty Square opened as one of the first federal housing projects for Black people, part of President Franklin Roosevelt's 'New Deal'. The community was prosperous and thriving, although physically walled off from an adjacent white residential area (Hannah-Jones 2017). Then local government built the I-95 motorway through a nearby low-income neighbourhood, Overtown. The displaced residents fled to Liberty Square followed by 'monster-sized concrete projects' and 'recalcitrant police officers' (Jones 2019: 99). In 1979, the beating and subsequent death of Arthur McDuffie at the hands of white police officers, who were later acquitted, sparked protests in Liberty City. Next, heroin and crack overwhelmed the neighbourhood, and crime rose steeply alongside defunding and the punitive 'war on drugs'. Thus, Jones summarizes Liberty City as a 'black space-place in which black people's experiences and feelings have been constructed and shaped by White supremacist structures', i.e., policy decisions around housing, policing and punishment (100).

The question of how one represents a neighbourhood like Liberty City on film is tied to questions of realism in filmmaking, the tension between aesthetic pleasure and true-to-life representation. Indeed, in the 1960s and 1970s, Blaxploitation films were accused of 'romanticiz[ing] the poverty and misery of the ghetto' and failing to capture the reality of the harsh conditions of life there (Guerrero 1993: 89). Susan Hayward writes that realism in film 'purports to give a direct and "truthful" view of the "real world" through the presentation it provides of the characters and their environment' (2000: 334). Realist films are grounded in concrete socio-political contexts and have a social mission to highlight the suffering or deprivation of particular communities, striving to accurately recreate the experiences and living conditions of the people they represent.

However, as Hayward points out, realist films 'tend to provide easy solutions', which can 'naturalize social problems and divisions and not provide any deep insight into causes' (2000: 334). While *Boyz N the Hood* does not offer facile solutions, the film does suggest two possible directions: departure and college, embodied in Tre, and a call for recognition of the suffering of the residents of this community through visual representation, an engagement that the film itself seems to enact. Debbie Olson goes so far as to suggest that representations of the hood in films such as *Boyz N the Hood* or *Menace II Society* 'suggest that the criminal environment is *made* criminal by the ontologically violent nature of the black men and boys who inhabit it' (2017: 138). Such a reading disregards the many ways in which hood films strive to show that it is the environment, the policing structures and social disregard, rather than any 'inherent' delinquency, that leads young men to crime. Nonetheless, there exists a tension in many realist films between representing the 'reality' of the community in question and the construction of these spaces as ones that cannot be reformed and must be forsaken in order for the individual to survive or thrive.

Furthermore, there are dangers in aestheticizing a world in which people exist in real hardship and social segregation. As Sohinee Roy writes in relation to the depiction of slums in films such as Danny Boyle's *Slumdog Millionaire* (2008), poverty and suffering can 'become a form of titillation [...] a picaresque narrative of adventure' (Roy 2016: 126). These films also risk a reception in which white audiences adopt an ethnographic gaze on the lives of others, viewing them as separate from their own worlds and experiences. Rendering this suffering as visually beautiful might mean that audiences ignore the wider systemic issues that have caused this structural inequality in the first place. As Jones asks, 'does *Moonlight* encourage most of its possible viewers to retain an image of the world of Liberty City – the structural, systemic material manifestation of the carceral continuum – *as a canvas*?' (2019: 100). The material reality of the segregated space of Liberty City becomes a painterly backdrop, beautiful scenery, against which an individual's story plays out. In this sense, the absence of white people in the film becomes problematic; as one viewer asked, 'who was bringing the crack-cocaine into the suburb of Miami?' (quoted in ibid. 94). In this reading, the beautification of Liberty City conceals more than it reveals about the operations of the structural racism and white power, which segregated the neighbourhood and flooded it with drugs.

For the most part, Liberty City in *Moonlight* is beautiful to behold. The film employs a cinematographic style that leans away from realism and toward the more self-reflexively expressive modes of arthouse filmmaking. From the outset of the film, Jenkins and Laxton play with the stark light, bright endless skies and scintillating colours of this part of south Florida. The scene in which the boys play football is overlaid with Mozart's 'Vesperae Solennes de Confessore, K. 339', which forms the only sound and then is sharply cut across by the sound of a freight train's blaring horn. Swinging and circular camera movements during the football scene create a sense of movement and fluidity in this space while the backdrop against which the boys play ball is a vast, untethered sky (see Figure 4.2). The use of colour throughout these sequences, discussed in more detail in the following section, is one of the most obvious ways in which the film generates its striking and visually pleasing aesthetic.

Figure 4.2 The boys play football against a vast Florida sky.

At the same time, it cannot be said that everything in the space of Liberty City is depicted as dazzling beauty and light. In many scenes, Jenkins shows beauty alongside destruction. In the opening sequence, Juan's assured introduction is undermined by a circling camera as he encounters one of his dealers, creating a sense of confinement and menace. When Little hides in the abandoned flat from his tormentors, dots of scintillating light are filmed alongside the discarded needles that litter the floor, and broken windows and doors frame the background. In the school, which is shot in vibrant cerulean tones, Chiron is frequently enclosed against the backdrop of walls, fences and doors. Moreover, in Part II of the film, the open spaces that had featured in Part I give way to a more restrictive framing of teenage Chiron: in one shot, he stands in the middle of the road, framed by its traffic markings, pavements, clothing lines and the walls of the buildings, with the broad Florida sky almost completely absent. Yet not only do Chiron's relationships with residents of Liberty City give him respite and support but the neighbourhood itself, it is suggested, contains these moments of beauty. Thus, when Kevin and Chiron meet at the beach, they discuss the breeze, emblematic of freedom and escape. Chiron says that you can feel the breeze in Liberty City, 'sometimes around the way, where we live, you can catch that same breeze. It comes through the hood and it's like everything stop for a second 'cause everybody just wanna feel it'.

These paradoxes in Liberty City, its depiction as beautiful and painful by turns, reflect both Jenkins and McCraney's memories of the area and, perhaps more pointedly, how they experience it now. Both men visited the neighbourhood in 2017 with *New York Times* journalist Nikole Hannah-Jones, and their reactions as they stand in one of its courtyards capture these contradictions. Jenkins says, 'this is the world of *Moonlight*. It's beautiful, right? When the sun comes out, it just pops', while McCraney adds, 'it is the confluence of madness and urban blight. Yet, it is incredibly beautiful. It is still a neighborhood' (quoted in Hannah-Jones 2017). In this sense, questions about *Moonlight*'s realism in terms of its depiction of the space of Liberty City come back to the conundrum of realistic *for whom*: Liberty City in *Moonlight* feels true for its creators, who are part of its historical fabric as former inhabitants.

Symbolism and sound (1): Colour

Jenkins describes *In Moonlight Black Boys Look Blue* as 'a visceral collection of memories' and 'a fever dream' (Pulver 2017). This dream-like quality is realized in the film in part through an intense utilization of colour, achieved by colourist Alex Bickel and Laxton's use of a high-definition digital anamorphic lens and widescreen CinemaScope. Moreover, as the title of the play suggests, colour generates meaning and symbolism in the film. Steven Peacock argues that colour can be applied to the study of film through the analysis of 'shifting patterns of colour, on repetitions, variation, and overlaps in meaning' (2010: xii). Peacock suggests that in considering colour, one should look at 'patterns' of colour: how colour plays out across the entire film and how colours interact with each other. Of particular importance to the consideration of colour in *Moonlight* is Peacock's attention to 'feeling in colour' and 'narrative-led colour coding' (5, 6): the ways in which colour is used to signify emotion and generate narrative meaning.

The three sections of *Moonlight* are distinctly colour coded. The entire opening section of the film uses the colours green and blue to convey positive moments in Chiron's life: Juan wears blue or green in most of the sequences in which he appears, as does Kevin, there are blue bins and sun loungers at the beach and the walls of Chiron's apartment are blue and green. Paula initially wears aquamarine tones, set against similar hues in their apartment living room wall, before she succumbs to her addiction. Pinks, reds and purples are also deployed as points of contrast in this opening section. Notably, Chiron himself spends much of this section in a fire-engine red T-shirt, which stands out in the natural greens and blues of Juan's garden and by the sea, reflecting the sense in which he feels different or apart from the world he navigates (see Figure 4.3). Neon pinks, purples and bright reds are also employed in the scene in which Paula's drug addiction worsens, and she shouts at Chiron: she stands in a red tank top, framed against the backdrop of a mauve wall with bright pink lintels on either side. In this sense, colour becomes a way to articulate Chiron's emotional life, with differing palettes signifying joy or fear.

The colours in Section II are not as vibrant as Section I, although this colour scheme still stands in sharp contrast to coming-of-age films set in the

Figure 4.3 Chiron surrounded by greens and blues in Part I.

city, where palates of grey, beige, brown and black are frequent. In Section II of the film, the colour yellow predominates. Chiron wears a flimsy check corn-coloured shirt for most of this section, mustard tones can be spotted in Teresa's tablecloth and buttercup yellow is seen in the lines on the road and the washing lines near Chiron's house. Bright industrial yellow also fills the sequence in which Chiron travels to the sea at night – subway poles and neon lights flash in the background (see Figure 4.4), as well as the dots of golden light that shimmer in the background during Kevin and Chiron's meeting on the beach. Yellow is associated with sunshine; however, in Section II, many of the scenes take place at night, in which the colour tone is artificial, in stark contrast to the numerous outdoor scenes in Section I. Yellow is also the colour of sickness and nausea, as well as warning. The fact that this section begins with a teacher's lesson on white blood cells and their role as defence in the body and ends with Chiron being beaten and then beating up Terrel in turn suggests that yellow, here, functions as a sign of ill-health and a premonition of danger. It may also reference Paula's worsening addiction, her queasy pallor and increasing sickness.

In the final section of the film, the colour schemes vary according to the sequence in question. In the scene when Kevin and Chiron reunite, red and brown tones are common in the diner, with caramel-toned leather banquettes, pillar-box red curtains, bright vermillion in the American flag, burgundy wine, a cherry-red gumball machine and brown and beige check wallpaper (see Figure 4.5). Red is, of course, the colour of love, but this colour scheme also lends a nostalgic, out-of-time feel to their reunion. Additionally, the reunion scene with Paula sees a return to the blues and greens that heralded happiness for Chiron in his childhood. However,

Figure 4.4 Industrial yellow fills the sequence in which Chiron travels to the sea at night in Part II.

Figure 4.5 Tones of red and brown fill the scene in the diner in Part III.

darker tones are more prevalent in the rest of the section, and black, brown and grey predominate in the opening passages, as we see Chiron go through the motions as a drug dealer in Atlanta. Kevin's call offers a glimpse of something brighter, as the shot-reverse-shot that captures their conversation also contrasts them starkly in terms of light and colour: Kevin wears a white shirt, holds a white phone and is shot against a bright background, while Chiron, now calling himself 'Black', is shot against a dark background, holding a black phone and wearing a black wave cap.

In terms of understanding the thematic significance of colour in the film, it is important to return to Juan's words to the child Chiron as they sit on the beach together. Juan's story of the old Cuban woman who says he looks blue under moonlight was an exhortation for Chiron not to let others, or the environment, define him. But blue also refers to melancholy, with a particular significance for the African American community because of the blues. The blues, a musical form originating in the Deep South in the 1860s and drawing on African spirituals and traditions, is a musical style in which experiences of pain, suffering and discrimination are narrated. For example, Curtis Mayfield draws these themes together in his song, 'We People Who Are Darker than Blue' (1970), whose opening lines are 'We people who are darker than blue / Are we gonna stand around this town / And let what others say come true?' Casey Hale notes that the song 'is a call to solidarity within the African American community, a plea for self-awareness and a renewed commitment to collective uplift' (Hale 2014: 36). It also connects to Chiron, who, in his transformation into an epitome of hegemonic hetero-sexuality, lets others define him. As Kannan et al. summarize, 'the hiding of his sexuality turned Black (Chiron), blue (sad)' (2018: 295).

Yet 'blue' in the film does not only refer to sadness and suffering; moreover, it is not blue in and of itself, but *blue under moonlight*, that is, 'in moonlight black boys look blue'. Taylor Barfield points out that 'blue' refers to 'an optical phenomenon in which dark, black skin appears blue under moonlight' (2017). The dark colour scheme of the final section of the film chimes with Chiron's reconfiguration of himself as Black: the name that Kevin gave him and the tough, normatively masculine persona he assumes. But from the outset of Section III, we see that there is a difference between Black in the daytime and in public, where he commands respect and even fear, and Black at night — where he experiences uncontrollable dreams, memories of fear and fantasies of queer desire. Many of Chiron's most significant emotional rites of passage take place at night: Paula's aggression, sexual intimacy with Kevin on the beach and emotional tenderness with Kevin in the diner and in his home.

This suggests that blue under moonlight is not, as Juan's words suggest, a false idea imposed by others but, rather, Chiron's real nature – within the scheme created by the film, that connects colour to emotion and selfhood. Indeed, Paula's exhortation to Chiron, that 'your heart ain't gotta be black like mine', seems to suggest that 'Black' is not his authentic self. Instead, two shots at the end of the film return Chiron to moonlight, to the ocean and to blueness. As he gets out of his car to go to Kevin's house, he glimpses the beach at night through a small gap in the seafront promenade, grey blue under the night sky. The final shot of the film, the child Chiron standing in front of the ocean just as he did many years before, recalls T.S. Eliot's words from *The Four Quartets*: 'We shall not cease from exploration / And the end of all our exploring / Will be to arrive where we started / And know the place for the first time' (1942). The film returns Chiron to being a Black boy in moonlight but, this time, with knowledge and understanding of the journey and with Kevin's tenderness and Paula's recovery to support his forward journey.

Symbolism and sound (2): Music

Speaking about Steven Spielberg's controversial rendering of Alice Walker's novel *The Color Purple*, Guerrero laments the fact that the film is punctuated by 'entertaining, folksy, musical interludes' and the same 'tired, Eurocentric movie music' on film soundtracks (1993: 51). He suggests, rather like Gates's delineation of beauty and high or low aesthetic styles, that Black music has been polarized as 'good' or 'bad': gospel and choir is acceptable, while jazz, rap and hip-hop is not. In *Moonlight*, Jenkins neither glorifies nor denounces any one musical genre but, instead, draws on a wide range of musical styles that combine an original classical score by Nicholas

Britell with hip-hop, rap, soul, R&B, classical and Mexican *huapango*. As Zaman summarizes, 'the soundtrack alone exemplifies a general rebellion against expectations' (2016: 42).

Nicholas Britell's score for the film captures the mood and pathos of the work. Tasha Robinson aptly observes that Britell's score gives the film a 'haunted but immediate quality that underscores the constant threat of violence without wringing it into melodramatic excess' (2017). Britell's score features three distinct but connecting themes to capture the three different stages of Chiron's life, played with a small chamber orchestra of piano and violin. 'Little's Theme' alternates between a D-major and G-minor chord, and this captures Chiron's tentative oscillation between moments of joy and sorrow in this opening section. A violin enters at the end, bouncing and played with a tentative uncertainty – reflecting Little's hesitancy and vulnerability. This track also features two pianos: one a grand fully in tune and the other an upright, slightly out of tune. These two pianos might reflect the purity of Little as a child on which the chaos of the 'out of tune' world is later imposed.

As Britell states 'one of the interesting challenges from a musical perspective is how do you provide a sense of cohesion across chapters while also allowing for transformation?' (quoted in Hirway 2017). Chiron's theme takes elements from Little's theme, such as the piano and violin, but pitches them down digitally to reflect his growing up, and they are played out of sync to capture the turbulence and pain of his teenage years. Britell and Jenkins decided to adopt the 'chopped and screwed' technique for the soundtrack at the fight with Kevin and the bullies. This is a method used in hip-hop that slows down the tempo of the song and uses stop-time and beat skips to create the effect of a chopped-up version of the track. The chopped and screwed version of Chiron's theme slows the track down and runs it through a vinyl filter so that it sounds like a record. Indeed, Clare Nina Norelli links this to the theme of water in *Moonlight*, stating that it sounds like Chiron's chopped and screwed theme is 'being heard underwater, as each individual note is ever-so-slightly distorted, unsteady in its resonance, and takes its time to reach our ears' (2017). This reflects the gravity of Kevin's betrayal, causing Chiron to sink, submerged by this deluge of disloyalty. Black's theme records the notes of Little's theme but is played in A-major by a cello octet that Britell then chopped and screwed to create a more assertive impression. However, the track manages also to capture sensitivity and vulnerability through the playing of the cellos using *tremolo* (bow shaking back and forth) and *pizzicato* (plucking of strings).

Jenkins's choice of diegetic, non-original music on the soundtrack of *Moonlight* speaks to the film's social, political and emotional meanings. The film opens, strikingly, with Boris Gardiner's 'Every N----r is a Star' (1974). This powerful sonic departure for the film initially appears as non-diegetic sound, before a close up reveals Juan turning off the radio in his car. If, as Guerrero notes, 'opening scenes often are used to express an ideological frame or orientation through which the spectator consumes the narrative' (1993: 32), this musical choice links Afro-Cuban Juan to a lineage of transnational and inter-generational Black artistry and storytelling. The track was made for the 1974 Blaxploitation film of the same title, directed by Calvin Lockhart. This is a classic soul track, and in the lyrics, pride is tinged with sadness as the singer laments '20 years I been on my own / hated and despised / no one to sympathize' before moving to the rousing, celebratory chorus (see Jones 2019: 101).

In a similar sense, Aretha Franklin's 'One Step Ahead' captures both the possibility of joy and a sorrow that threatens to follow. Played when Little observes his mother taking drugs as a child and when Black enters the diner to meet Kevin, the song is ostensibly about the fear of being let down by an unreliable lover. However, for Bruce, there are wider social and political meanings to be taken from the track. He argues that the song shows the 'precarious interstice' between '"misery" right behind you and loneliness just ahead' (2019: 355). He continues:

> *Moonlight* illuminates the lives of people who live 'one step ahead of misery', one check ahead of poverty, one puff away from addiction, one schoolyard brawl away from expulsion, one taunt away from mental breakdown, one conviction away from a life sentence. (356)

Goodie Mob's 'Cell Therapy' (1995) also deals with political themes, such as gentrification, mass incarceration and the group even suggest the song foreshadowed lockdown life during the 2020 pandemic (Shaw 2020).

Jenkins says that he 'wanted the music to express the consciousness of the character, and not necessarily the propulsion of the plot' (Boyce Gillespie 2017: 60). The soundtrack in the film also provides a romantic backdrop to Kevin and Chiron's relationship, particularly in the final section of the film. In the scene in which we see Chiron driving down a highway at sunset, travelling south to see Kevin, 'Cucurrucucú Paloma' by Caetano Veloso plays on the soundtrack. This is a song of longing and lovesickness sung by a man who waits for a woman to return. The song evokes a heterosexual unrequited love sung in the third person, but it also has queer cinematic precursors: it is played in *Happy Together* and in Pedro Almodóvar's *Talk to Her* (2002). Alexandra Reznik offers an excellent discussion of other musical choices in this third section of the film, including Erykah Badu's 'Tyrone' and 'Our Love' by The Edge of Daybreak. In the former, a woman tells a man that she just wants to be with him, prefiguring, as Reznik suggests, the fact that Chiron has never been touched by anyone but Kevin (2019:

118). 'Our Love', a song about waiting for a lover, was written by a group formed inside Powhatan Correctional Center in 1979. While earlier tracks such as 'Tyrone' and 'Cucurrucucú Paloma' have gendered, heterosexual pronouns, 'Our Love' and 'Hello Stranger' do not, suggesting for Reznik a move from heterosexual frameworks of expression toward allowing 'the lyrics to articulate desire between two Black men' (119).

Reznik further argues that music is used in this third section of *Moonlight* to queer Chiron's overt expression of heterosexual masculinity. For example, when Chiron pulls up outside Kevin's diner, the thick bass of 'Classic Man' saturates the audible field, highlighting his transition from nervous boy to epitome of hardened masculinity. However, as Reznik points out, this must be read within the context of a man who has travelled hundreds of miles to see another man after more than a decade of separation. Drawing on the work of Riggs, Reznik highlights how *Tongues Untied* also provides ironic sound–music disjunctions in its exploration of the silences surrounding Black male homosexuality (2019: 117). Indeed, Kevin later teases Chiron about the song, asking with a hint of innuendo, grinning as he says, 'ride dirty, huh?' 'Classic Man' for Reznik 'summons the audience to begin to see how the desire between Black men manifests and exists in plain sight even within a heteronormative power structure' (116), echoing Johnson's discussion of 'quare' in Chapter 3. Alongside all these musical references and undertones, Reznik points out that the most intimate scenes between Chiron and Kevin are conducted in silence, apart from the sound of the ocean and the breeze. Just as music is multifaceted in that it 'can reinforce heteronormativity, sexism, racism, classism, *and* it can be liberating and provide sustenance' (120), so too can silence function as both a signifier of intimacy and a sign of oppression.

Conclusion

This analysis of *Moonlight*'s formal properties highlights the ways in which the film straddles multiple traditions, forms and styles that are sometimes viewed as oppositional. Thus, it incorporates the linear and cyclical narrative tracks identified by Diawara in relation to arthouse filmmaking. *Moonlight* makes Liberty City beautiful but without glossing over the harsh conditions that poverty and segregation impose on its residents. Similarly, music in the film refuses to be neatly categorized, as classical exists alongside soul, hip-hop and chopped and screwed techniques while patterns of colour encode emotions both agreeable and painful, expressing the evolution of character and themes.

5   Empathy, universality and Black boyhood in *Moonlight*

This chapter untangles some of the ideas around specificity, universality and empathy that occur and recur in the critical reception of *Moonlight*, and then, considering the representation of Black boyhood in the film, offers a historical overview as well as a detailed analysis of space, being and the three-part structure. The film's appeal to viewers, who identified strongly with some or all of Chiron's experiences as a minority ethnic and gay youth growing up in a marginalized community, suggests that such representations are long overdue. However, Chiron's story also has many of the characteristics of the conventional youth film: conflict with a parental figure, the discovery of an older mentor and friend, isolation and bullying at school, a first encounter with love and a quest to discover his true self. *Moonlight* is at once highly specific to Black queer youth cultures and communities while, at the same time, the great tenderness with which Jenkins treats his subject matter can evoke for audiences of varying age groups and backgrounds the bittersweet trials, tribulations and joys of childhood and youth.

Empathy, audiences and *Moonlight*: Between the universal and the specific

Moonlight received almost universal critical praise, across political boundaries and among mainstream and independent media. In many cases, the positive reception of *Moonlight* is tied to the feelings of empathy that the film evokes in viewers, most particularly for the central character, Chiron. The *Washington Post* writes that filmgoers can 'finally see a perfect film, one that exemplifies not only the formal and aesthetic capabilities of a medium at its most visually rich, but a capacity for empathy and compassion that reminds audiences of one of the chief reasons why we go to movies' (Hornaday 2017). The British right-wing daily the *Telegraph* evokes the film's 'grace' and its 'compassionate' storyline (Collin 2016), while *Christianity Today* calls *Moonlight* 'a rewarding exercise in Christian

DOI: 10.4324/9780429055294-5

empathy', acknowledging that even though the film is 'at odds with a biblical sexual ethic', it may be 'worth the discomfort' (Roark 2017). Critics in the liberal press are at pains to stress the film's universal appeal, an appeal that is almost always grounded in ideas of empathy and love. For example, Mark Kermode writes of *Moonlight* that it is 'a five-star symphony of love' (2017), while Benjamin Lee argues that *Moonlight* proves that the so-called 'racial empathy gap' may be overcome, whereby white audiences are presumed not to be able to identify with non-white characters (2017c).

However, the film is deeply tied to the emotional and social experiences of particular viewers, notably Black and minority ethnic and LGBT and queer. Other critics lauded *Moonlight*'s ability to be, in the words of the *Atlantic* writer David Sims, 'both specific and sweeping', and he cites the scene between Chiron and Kevin on the beach as one example of Jenkins's skill in rendering intimacy 'at once exclusive to the couple and yet utterly universal' (2016). Other critics echoed this terminology of the specific and the universal precisely. Thus, in the *Evening Standard*, *Moonlight* is read as 'a form of poetry, at once utterly specific and universal' (Anon. 2016), while *ABC News* says 'Jenkins created a specific story that could resonate universally' (Fisher 2017). Kristopher Tapley, a writer for *Variety*, tweeted, '*Moonlight*'s specificity reaches such a quantum level that it miraculously becomes universal' (quoted in Bastién 2017). Even Jenkins himself adopts the language of the universal and the specific in describing *Moonlight*'s appeal, while remaining attentive to the film's particular relationship to Blackness: 'the movie is about very specific characters, in a very specific neighbourhood, going through very specific ordeals. In that specificity there's something universal, but also there's a statement on the black experience' (quoted in Scott 2016). Indeed, ideas of empathy were so central to the discussion of the film in mainstream media that Camilla Long, who called *Moonlight* 'a story told countless times' (Long 2017), was then herself pitied for her apparent 'struggle to feel for those who aren't like you' (Shoard 2017).

Peter Verstraten argues that *Moonlight* is the 'mass art' film of the 2010s, defining mass art films as those that 'find a balance, quite effortlessly, between box-office and aesthetic success, and thereby transgress the gap between high and low culture' (2019). These are films that win Academy Awards yet are also popular on festival circuits and are often screened in multiplexes and arthouse theatres – films that woo critics as well as the general public. Verstraten states that mass art films generally feature a character who is a kind of 'Everyman', a relatively blank character with 'no particular innate qualities'. What is unusual about *Moonlight* as mass art film, then, is that Chiron is an 'Everyman' figure but without adopting the 'empty' characteristics of many protagonists of such commercial and critical successes. As Verstraten writes, 'Jenkins presents [Chiron] in all his complexity, inviting us to connect to him *as if* he were "one of us"' (2019; emphasis added). Yet many viewers did, indeed, feel that Chiron was 'one of them', as demonstrated in the discussion of the film's reception in Chapter 3. Indeed, while Verstraten does recognize Chiron's 'highly particularized' background, there is an implicit assumption in his interpretation of *Moonlight* that the viewer will be different from Chiron, as though the usual white, American and middle-class 'Everyman' character of mass art films always appeals to audiences.

When critics evoke the universal, as Farihah Zaman points out, 'this particular universe tends to belong on screen to the white, straight middle class' (2016). For Zaman, the universal constitutes a 'shared human experience', but one that is rarely experienced in cinema through the prism of Black characters and filmic worlds. Other critics question the category of the universal altogether: Bastién argues that themes in *Moonlight*, such as loneliness, desire and identity may be shared, but 'to say that *Moonlight* is universal ignores how these experiences are filtered through identity' (2017). The evocation of a universal viewing experience when it comes to *Moonlight* seeks to centre the presumed white and heterosexual viewer and account for the film's popularity among 'mass' audiences. Indeed, Bastién suggests that 'the narrative around *Moonlight* as […] ultimately a universal story is a way for Hollywood and its white power structures to adopt the success of the film as its own' (2017).

Moreover, theorists of visual culture have cautioned against the reliance on a notion of 'universal' subjectivity. Richard Dyer explains how such ideas of the universal and 'universal humanity' have been co-opted to centre white experience: 'they/we function as a human norm. Other people are raced, we are just people' (1997: 1), in which 'just people' functions as a synonym for 'just human'. bell hooks notes a certain 'rage' among white students when attention is drawn to their race: 'their rage erupts because they believe that all ways of looking that highlight difference subvert the liberal belief in a universal subjectivity (we are all just people) that they think will make racism disappear' (2015: 167). Janine Jones reiterates the taken-for-granted nature of the association with whiteness and humanity in her study of *Moonlight*: 'the symbolic economy of whiteness does not require an erasure or an addition […] No need to say they are white, and no need to say that they are H/human' (2019: 95). The evocation of the 'universal' or the 'just human' can function as a mode of negation in relation to the very specific experience of inhabiting a particular (raced, gendered, sexed, abled) body in a particular socio-political space.

Jones writes persuasively of the ways in which critics, in many cases, divest *Moonlight* of its specificity, its Blackness and queerness, in order to praise the film. She cites A.O. Scott's *New York Times* review as a particular case in point, in which Scott suggests that 'to describe "Moonlight" […] as a movie about growing up poor, black, and gay would be […] inadequate […and] downright misleading' (Scott 2016a; Jones 2019: 95). Jones also cites John Anderson in the *Wall Street Journal* who praises the film's 'chaste' approach to Chiron and Kevin's teenage sexual encounter, erasing its queer specificity: 'what's important isn't gayness, necessarily, or even sex, but the realization of who you really are' (2016; Jones 2019: 95). In their tendency to negate or underplay the film's relationship to the specific identities it depicts, these critics highlight a quest for empathy *in spite of* difference. Jones states that 'black people tend to disappear in human empathy projects' (ibid.), an assertion that is borne out by Sims's interpretation of the film: 'this is not an "issue" film that's mainly "about" race or sexuality; this is a humane movie, one that's looking to prompt empathy and introspection most of all' (2016). In Sims's interpretation, the 'issues' of the film – its Blackness and queerness – struggle to co-exist with a notion of the 'humane' and empathy.

However, in the midst of all these critical calls to empathy may lie a lack of interrogation of what the term actually means and how it can function in different socio-political contexts. Roger Ebert famously called film 'a machine that generates empathy', because film 'helps us to identify with the people who are sharing this journey with us' (2018). Empathy is a term that easily slides into correlatives like sympathy, compassion and pity. Indeed, in one of the only negative reviews of the film by a Black male critic, Armond White in the *National Review*, pity rather than empathy is evoked. White calls Chiron a 'black, gay statistic' and says that the film 'pleads for pity for a gay, black character, and pity is always for the weak' (2016). White is a conservative critic, and his use of the term 'pity' rather than 'empathy' speaks to a growing trend among right-wing commentators to denigrate the 'snowflake generation' and their engagement with social justice movements that highlight minority groups (see Morris 2020). Indeed, released as it was in 2016, at the end of the Obama presidency and at the dawn of the Trump era, Jenkins even views *Moonlight* as a kind of barometer of national feeling, stating 'I think this movie is a test of people's empathy at this moment in America's history' (quoted in Whipp 2016).

Writing about emotion and tragedy, Susan Feagin notes that one of the pleasures of the form is the feeling of shared empathy, or pity, for suffering characters. In short, the spectator feels pleasure at being the kind of person who feels pity in the face of human suffering. The feeling of empathy 'shows what we care for, and in showing us we care for the welfare of human beings and that we deplore the immoral forces that defeat them, it reminds us of our common humanity' (1998: 307). Here, Feagin is in the register of the 'H/human' and 'just people', critiqued by scholars such as Jones (2019) and Dyer (1997). Indeed, Sara Ahmed is careful to point out that when it comes to looking at the suffering of another, the reader and victim, or viewer and victim, are not in 'a relation of equivalence'. This lack of equivalence is, of course, magnified when observer and sufferer, subject and object, are in a hierarchical relation by virtue of class, race, gender, ability or other characteristics. Ahmed argues that the experience of pain creates a distance: 'we feel sad *about* their suffering, an "aboutness" that ensures they remain the object of "our feeling"' (2014: 21).

Empathy, therefore, can divide the subject and object of feeling as well as unite them. An ethical response to witnessing the pain of another, in reality or representation, Ahmed argues, 'involves being open to being affected by that which one cannot know or feel' (30). Rather than 'fully comprehending' the suffering of another, one remains attentive to the distance between another's experience and one's own. This idea is echoed in scholarly writing on empathy in the classroom, particularly in relation to artistic texts. Polina Kukar, for example, is critical of approaches that invite students to 'imagine themselves "in the shoes" of someone else' and, thus, encourage a feeling of a 'common humanity' (2016: 2). As she notes, the idea of a 'common humanity' often erases structural power differences between college students and some of the lives they encounter in the texts they study. Instead, she invites educators to consider a 'pedagogy of discomfort' in which students are encouraged to mine their own relation to the suffering of another, in which an 'encounter with another in an educational setting does not yield concrete knowledge of that other, but merely an awareness and respect for the difference' (4).

This is similar to Ahmed's evocation of an empathy that retains a distance between self and other, that accepts difference in the absence of similarity. It also recalls Bastién's forthright critique of white critical responses to *Moonlight*, in which 'the discussion around *Moonlight*'s supposed universality betrays a stunning lack of empathy by white and straight critics that suggest the only Black stories that matter are the ones they can see themselves in' (2017). As she continues, 'stories of Black people don't need to be universal in order to have broader relevance' (ibid.). One can feel empathy for the situation of another without having to view oneself as similar or the same as that other. Perhaps the most difficult empathy lies in viewing the suffering and humanity of those who are different from us, those with whom we disagree; even those we may not like. An ethics of empathy in cinema might be one in which 'you don't need to directly see yourself in a film to empathize with the world it creates' (Bastién 2017).

Indeed, Jenkins drew on feelings of both commonality and difference in his decision to make the film. He acknowledges the deep kinship he felt with the character in every aspect of his identity apart from his sexuality. As a straight man, he initially had some reservations about making the film: 'can I, as a straight man, really tell this story fully – in the way it needs to be told?' (quoted in Pulver 2017). However, he goes on to note that he approached the character's sexuality from the position of an 'ally'. Thus, the position of empathy that the film itself departs from is one in which the easier identifications of sameness lead to a greater understanding of points of difference. He writes that he 'wanted to very actively and deeply access [his] own empathy, to create this path of empathy for these characters'. He notes that *Moonlight* was not only about 'stir[ring] feelings in people', but also about creating a film that in itself would be 'an active ally for anyone in the world feeling the things these characters feel, no matter where they are or who they are or what their circumstance' (quoted in Myers 2016).

It is worth noting that Jenkins here describes the film's allyship in terms of shared feeling, thus, emphasizing the emotions of loneliness, longing, exclusion and love (both pleasurable and painful) that the film eloquently evokes. Certainly, when I teach this film to diverse student groups, their first responses to the film cite its powerful expression of these emotions, many of which relate to the film's depiction of Chiron as a child. Therefore, I want to turn to the film's vision of childhood to consider the ways in which *Moonlight* navigates this period of human life. It is a stage of life at once considered to be powerfully universal and yet lived very differently between individuals – a state of vulnerability that inspires great love and great neglect – and, in cinematic terms, a time for which feelings of empathy are most easily evoked. In the following section, I first look at how *Moonlight* engages with some of the perennial themes of childhood, such as universality, innocence and vulnerability. I show how these themes are context specific or, to recall Bastién's (2017) terms, 'filtered through identity' in that they can play out very differently for Black boys in America. This points toward the revolutionary power of having this story about a Black child resonate empathically with audiences.

Childhood on film and Black boyhood denied

Although many reviews mention the representation of childhood in *Moonlight*, few emphasize its centrality to the story of the film. The film begins and ends on the image of the child Chiron, highlighting the cyclical narrative and the significance of that image to the film's deeper meanings. In the speech that he was meant to give at the Oscars, Jenkins intended to say: 'Tarell and I are that boy. We are Chiron' (Pallotta 2018). Their identification with the central character is deep and profound, and it is arguably this identification and the emotional authenticity that it lends to the narrative that makes the depiction of childhood in *Moonlight* so affecting. Their re-creation of their childhoods through the filmmaking process chimes with Hugh Cunningham's declaration that notions of childhood come from adults imagining and re-imagining it, 'inventing it, in order to make sense of their world' (2006: 12). McCraney has also emphasized the ways in which the film 'preserved the story, the look, the feel and the sounds of his childhood' (quoted in Del Barco 2016), highlighting its proximity to the autobiographi-cal, not only in terms of narrative but also aesthetic choices.

Trevante Rhodes, who plays the adult Chiron notes, '[*Moonlight*] does speak to so many people, and everyone who watches the film leaves feeling like there was a part of them in it' (Merry 2016). Given that the experience of childhood is often remembered, eliciting intense adult emotion, it is possible that many of the audience members who see a part of themselves in *Moonlight* are identifying with the figure of the child. Indeed, although Fragoso says that *Moonlight* is about a 'tragic childhood' (2016), the account of Chiron's youth that the film offers is much more complex than a simple portrait of sorrow and suffering. Indeed, it might be argued that all childhoods, viewed from the perspective of adulthood, are in some way tragic, in the sense that they inspire pity and fear in the adult who gazes back at their own past vulnerability, con-templating the myriad ways in which the physical, emotional and material exposure of childhood could have been, or was, exploited.

Childhood has frequently been evoked as a universal, shared human experience. As Neil Sinyard writes, 'childhood is the great universal theme' (1995: 44), and Debbie Olson notes that 'discourse about children or child-hood is often framed in universal terms, that is, "The Child"' (Olson 2018: x). Early scholarship on childhood frequently spoke of this stage of life in the singular – childhood rather than childhoods. Works such as Philip Ariès's *Centuries of Childhood* (1962) and Lloyd DeMause's *The History of Childhood* (1974) trace changing social and political attitudes to childhood across time but tended to view ideals of European childhood as the model or basis for their examinations. The evocation and defence of the 'innocence of children' is central to many representations of childhood, encompassing the notion that children should be protected from adult knowledge about sex, death and violence. The loss of that childish innocence forms the backbone of many coming-of-age narratives, from *ET* (Spielberg 1982) to *Stand By Me*.

Social fears about the loss of that innocence means that the figure of the child in film, as Vicky LeBeau argues, has been used to embody the anxie-ties of modern life (2008). If the child remains innocent, the world in which he or she exists is itself pure; if the child is corrupted, it is symptomatic of a corrupt world. In a similar vein, Phil Powrie argues that 'the stand-ard Romantic view of the child is one of almost pre-lapsarian innocence' (2005: 343). Nonetheless, he suggests that representations of children can look back through either a utopic or dystopic lens, whereby the viewer either laments the loss of sepia-tinted innocence or shudders gratefully that their childhood did not carry such anguishes (ibid.). Thus, one witnesses the dichotomization of the figure of the child, particularly in film, in which representations range from the quasi-angelic (Annie, Shirley Temple, Harry Potter) to the downright monstrous (Damien in *The Omen* (Donen 1976), Regan in *The Exorcist* (Friedkin 1973)).

The figure of the child, thus, carries cultural weight, becoming a barometer of fears and fantasies about the past and the future. Lee Edelman describes the particular investments in children as 'reproductive futurism', in which 'the Child has come to embody for us the telos of the social order and come to be seen as the one for whom that order is held in trust' (2011: xi). The widely held and socially endorsed notion of The Child as investment, as future-oriented security for both the society and the individual who seek to live on in genes or values through the next generation(s), ignores the reality that many living children are not valued nearly as much as The Child of universalist imagination. Moreover, the image of the white, blonde, angelic and middle-class child of nostalgic and utopic representations has little in common with the lived experiences of many children. As Jack Halberstam reminds us, childhood can be 'a time of brutality, cruelty, and violence' (2018: 58). Children are cruel to each other and to adults as they navigate their own power, desires, abilities and the mores and morals of the adults around them.

Cruelty in childhood comes in the form not only of the petty nastiness and sometimes physical violence that children can inflict on one another but also from the social and political conditions to which particular children are subject. A film like Lynne Ramsay's *Ratcatcher* (1999) captures the ways in which children hurt one another while setting this brutality against the backdrop of vicious poverty in 1970s Glasgow. Ramsay, thus, highlights how social cruelty intersects with interpersonal cruelty through the figure of the child. Jenkins, who has cited Ramsay as an artistic inspiration, offers a similar intertwining of personal and socio-political struggle. Thus, in staging Chiron's childhood as he confronts structural racism, social disenfranchisement and homophobia, Jenkins forces the viewer to recognize the particular vulnerabilities of Black boys, challenging formative images of childhood in cinema. More recently, works such as *Get Out*, Childish Gambino's 'This is America' (2018), Melina Matsoukas's *Queen and Slim* (2019), George Tillman Jr.'s *The Hate U Give* (2018) and the episode Jenkins directed for the series *Dear White People* (Season 1, Episode V, 2016) highlight the perils that Black boys and young men face in contemporary America.

In 1955, the murder of Emmett Till, a Chicago boy visiting family in Mississippi, by a white lynch mob shocked many across the US and was credited with invigorating the Civil Rights movement. Yet, moving into the twenty-first century, with the increasing availability of camera phones, shock continues as more and more videos emerge of African Americans being shot at, attacked and killed by the police. The epidemic of police violence against Black people has been brought to the fore by the Black Lives Matter movement. Yet, the deaths of Black boys such as Tamir Rice (12 years old) and Trayvon Martin (17 years old), among others, also raise troubling questions not only about policing, brutality and racism but also the perception of Black boyhood in the United States. Rice and Martin were boys, yet, in each case, emphasis was laid on the fact that they did not 'look' or 'act' like boys. In the case of Rice, the initial 911 caller stressed both that Rice was likely a juvenile and that the gun was likely fake, yet police officers 'mistook' a toy gun for a real gun and shot the boy within less than 2 seconds of arriving at the scene (see Shaffer 2019 (2014); Blackwell 2019 (2014)).

This inability – or perhaps, more accurately, wilful blindness – to viewing Black boys as boys speaks to the ways in which Black boyhood is, according to Michael J. Dumas and Joseph Derrick Nelson, both 'socially unimagined and unimaginable' (2016: 27). Dumas and Nelson argue that instead of focusing on what Black boys are, society focuses on what they become, Black adult men, who are themselves subject to damaging discourses about criminality and violence. Black boys are, thus, 'often perceived to be older than they really are and are often judged as less innocent than their white peers' (29), subject to greater disciplinary controls in schools, greater criminalization of their actions and, ultimately, as the cases above suggest, greater state and social violence. This 'adultification', they argue, is part of a 'process of dehumanization […] a construction of the Other as not human, as less than human, and therefore undeserving of the emotional and moral recognition accorded to those whose shared humanity is understood' (ibid.). Simone C. Drake echoes these sentiments, arguing that Black boys have been persistently subject to what she calls 'discourses of crisis', and she criticizes America's difficulty in 'permitting black boys the opportunity to simply be boys and not pathological deviants' (2016: 448).

If African Americans in film were subject to stereotypical representation by white Hollywood, Black children on screen were perhaps even more stereotyped and misrepresented. For, as Halberstam notes, childhood itself 'is the condition of *being represented by* adults' (2018: 57). Thus, Black children were subject to a representation twice removed: by adults and through the lens of whiteness. Robin Bernstein cites the ways in which 'white children became constructed as tender angels while Black children were libelled as unfeeling, non-innocent, non-children' during colonialism, slavery and the Jim Crow era (2001: 29). The stereotypes of Black women and men in film also extended to Black children through the figures of the so-called 'pickaninny' and 'Sambo'. Bogle describes the character as 'a harmless, little screwball creation[s] whose eyes popped, whose hair stood on end with the least excitement, and whose antics were pleasant and diverting' (1994: 7).

Indeed, ideas of innocence themselves were and are racially coded. An early instance of the contrasting of white childhood innocence and Black childhood dehumanization was the hit melodrama *Uncle Tom's Cabin*, in which angelic Eva is contrasted with naughty Topsy. Blackness was associated not with innocence but with childish naiveté; one only has to consider the figure of Uncle Remus in Disney's 1946 *Song of the South* (Jackson) or the innumerable dance numbers performed by the tiny blond Shirley Temple with Bill 'Bojangles' Robinson to see cinema's attempts to associate Blackness with childishness. This contrasting of innocence as purity for white people with innocence as ignorance for Black people is outlined extensively in Mary Louise Pratt's 2008 study, *Imperial Eyes: Writing and Transculturation*. White Europeans constructed ideas of innocence and childhood in their own image, and as Olson notes, this resulted in 'the persistent visual presentation of the black child as a non-child' (2017: 14).

Olson traces a transmutation in the figure of the Black child from 1955 onward, emerging, not coincidentally, with the growing Civil Rights movement in the US. Leaving behind the 'screwball' stereotype, the Black child emerges as a problem, a 'disturbing depiction of the violent, criminal, urban black male youth, which quickly became the stock image for black boys' (2017: 45). Beginning with the film *The Blackboard Jungle* (Brooks 1955), Olson tracks the development of these twin themes – urban setting and criminality – in depictions of Black youth through the decades, in films such as *Dangerous Minds* (Smith 1995) and *Fresh* (Yakin 1995). By moving the figure of the Black child from pre-teen years to adolescence, such films contribute to the 'adultification' outlined by Drake and Dumas and Nelson while also giving an image to the discourses of criminalization and discipline that structure dominant accounts of Black youth, contributing to the persistent invisibility of the Black child in film and the unwillingness to see Black childhood as such.

Moonlight: Illuminating Black boyhood

Moonlight offers a nuanced, poignant and, at times, joyful representation of Black boyhood. Jenkins does not elide the very real material and familial hardships that Chiron faces, such as bullying and his mother's addiction, and neither does he deny his child character moments of love, hope and pleasure. He creates this portrait of a childhood grounded in a specific time, space and experience, but at the same time, tentatively, he goes so far as to call aspects of this experience universal:

> I hate to use the word *universally,* but you're universally in the throes of childhood [...] You don't typically expect this narrative of this poor black boy in the slums of Miami struggling with his sexuality. And now it's just about being a child. You have all this life coursing through you.
>
> (quoted in Swanson 2016)

Jenkins views something in childhood as universal, which, while acknowledging its many variants and differences, critics and audiences seem to share and to which the consistent popularity of coming-of-age narratives would seem to attest. While I certainly do not want to suggest that all audiences feel empathy for child Chiron or feel empathy in an equal manner for him, in the following sections, I argue that *Moonlight* offers a vision of Black childhood that is legible or, to draw on Dumas and Nelson's terms, that is 'imagined and imaginable' through the evocation of space, being and the three-part structure.

One of the ways in which *Moonlight* counteracts dominant images of Black boyhood is through its evocation of outdoor, natural space. This is significant because films about childhood often use rural spaces and symbolic distinctions between countryside and city to evoke nostalgia, the supposed naturalness of childhood and childhood innocence. Moreover, the shift in images of Black children in cinema from the 1950s onward was one that moved from rural spaces, often the plantation, to the urban 'jungle'. This furthered an association of whiteness with nature and purity and Blackness with the crime, dangers and moral dissipation of the city. As Olson summarizes, 'in the white imagination, people of colour [...represent] an urban, "alien" environment, and the white landscape of rurality is aligned with naiveness and the absence of evil or danger' (2017: 52). Movingly, this image of the perfect rural childhood is evoked by Coates, who describes it as the epitome of the American Dream, one that seemed denied to boys like him: 'I knew ... that this fear was connected to the Dream out there, to the unworried boys, to pie and pot roast, to the white fences and green lawns nightly beamed into our television sets' (2015: 29).

Moonlight situates Chiron in natural spaces, and in the film, we first meet him running through green fields. He is running to flee from bullies, and Jenkins films this scene using an out of focus lens, that swings from side to side capturing bright blurs of green and blue. He runs inside a building, transitioning from natural to man-made space in which gleaming, almost pointillistic dots of colour provide a contrast to the violent banging at the door. There are needles on the floor and boarded up windows, and this constructed space is shown not to be Chiron's 'natural' environment, but rather a manifestation of urban blight that is alien, forbidding and dangerous. Juan arrives to rescue him, cracking open a window through which daylight floods the room. Indeed, Chiron is pictured at several moments waiting outside Juan's house, surrounded by lush leafy plants and grass, thus, associating the man who helps and takes care of him with plant life and greenery.

Yet natural spaces in *Moonlight* are not fetishized nostalgically as pure and innocent but, rather, are depicted simply as spaces of freedom, a freedom that contains both the fear of flight from bullies and the freedom to run and play. The scene in which the boys play football amid a vast green field captures childhood as a space of both exclusion and connection. The camera circles around a group of boys, hunched over a ball made of rolled up paper, and as classical music mingles with the sound of the horn of a passing freight train, Chiron wanders off alone. Kevin follows him, and they tussle on the grass against the backdrop of a vast sky. Similarly, the scene in which Juan teaches Chiron to swim is both euphoric and a little bit frightening: the camera is almost submerged in the water, and we get a child's eye view of the undulating waves, the threat of submergence, shot through with the exhilarating and frightening feeling of almost being out of one's depth (see Figure 5.1). This sense of precarity, the fear and excitement that attends a new experience in childhood and how easily such an experience can tip from joy to fear or vice versa, is captured in the undulating violin track that rises and falls in arpeggio, contrasting Juan's encouraging, enthusiastic support of his small friend with Chiron's trepidation.

Figure 5.1 A child's-eye view of the undulating waves in the swimming sequence.

In this way, Jenkins undoes some of the associations between childhood and natural space as a relation of simple pleasure. Yet he also situates a Black boy concretely within these natural outdoor spaces – spaces that he himself experienced as a boy, and spaces that existed alongside, and not apart from, urban deprivation:

> I got the opportunity to take my memory and put it on screen: in Miami, you're often adrift, you're just walking through these massive spaces. [...] This is a rough neighbourhood and we're really poor, and there's nothing to eat on Fridays, but shit, there's this huge field I've got. I'm going to go out and run and play [...] There's so much greenery and open sky, so we wanted to reflect that.
>
> (quoted in Rapold 2016)

These scenes come to depict the ways in which memories of childhood are filtered through space. Crucially, these images provide a template for childhood exploration, one that is neither idealized nor vilified. For, as Dumas and Nelson note, 'with regard to Black boys, the public and even scholars, to some degree, become preoccupied with order and discipline, paying minimal or no attention to boys' experiences of play or peer friendships or caring [...] Childhood itself must be put aside, and these boys must become men' (2016: 35). *Moonlight* does not only show Chiron's struggles but also his play and being both excluded and loved. These images show 'what childhood means – that is, children are worthy of protection and are entitled to play and discover' (30).

Karen Lury also draws distinctions between 'showing' and 'seeing' in films about childhood, stating that 'the child encourages us to *see* the world differently' (2005: 308). 'Showing' refers to a 'purposeful' and 'directed' gaze, that is 'part of a narrative which links cause to effect' (ibid.). This is a vision that is grounded in historical and political time and is evident in films such as *Boyz N the Hood*, which keeps the child protagonists bound by a world that is spatially and temporally coherent. *Moonlight*, by contrast, does not treat its setting as incidental, but incidental in a political sense, because it seeks to offer the viewer a vision of Chiron's childhood not through the eyes of adults who classify and categorize but, rather, as an 'emotional geography', a sequence of experiences not connected primarily by cause and effect or time and place but, rather, by emotion. Thus, Lury suggests that the child sees in a way that is different to adults, 'a sense in which effects (what is seen) are closer to affect (what is felt)' (ibid.).

Moonlight captures this childlike overlapping of sight and emotion through its cinematography, most notably the use of point of view shots, shaky cameras, out of focus shots, colour and sound–image disjunctions.

Figure 5.2 The scene in which Paula shouts at Chiron, filmed from his perspective.

For example, in the scenes in which Paula's addiction worsens, she angrily shouts at him, but the sound is drowned out by music and she is framed in slightly neon pinks and purples in the hallway of their home (see Figure 5.2). This evokes a sense of a memory or a dream in which the wordless, unheard screams and the surreal lighting serve principally as a vector for Chiron's feeling of fear. This focus on 'seeing' rather than 'showing' is significant because it invites the viewer to focus on who Chiron is and how he feels in these moments of childhood rather than who he will become. As Dumas and Nelson point out, 'we have created a world in which Black boys cannot be' (2016: 28). Discourses of adultification, the slippage of the language of boy into man, create a situation in which it becomes 'important to be able to see what boyhood looks like' (Drake 2016: 448). Indeed, according to Dumas and Nelson, one of the problems of 'the "boys into men" discourse' is that it can 'devolve into a defense of a patriarchal Black masculinity', one in which alternative subjectivities, such as 'Black gender-nonconforming and gay/queer/questioning boys' (2016: 39) can become further overlooked or even denigrated.

One of the discoveries of childhood is the discovery of oneself as a body in the world, and *Moonlight* adopts a light touch in exploring the child Chiron's sexuality, one that stresses the importance of being in the world without the burden of becoming. Chiron's sexuality is hinted at in a number of scenes, such as an extended glance between himself and Kevin after they scuffle on the grass. Another short scene, which almost slips by unnoticed, is the image of Chiron's dancing in school. We watch him from behind amid a group of boys and girls as he watches himself in the mirror, mounted on a pink wall, twisting and turning happily in time to the music. Chiron's awareness of his queerness comes from others who want to name what he will, or may, become. There is Paula, who laughs at how he walks and asks Juan if he wants to raise a child like Chiron. It is also in the off-camera names that other children call him, namely 'faggot'. Chiron repeats this word to Juan, asking the older man what it means and whether he, Chiron, is one. Juan not only rejects this word as one that is 'used to make gay people feel bad', but he also rejects the imperative for Chiron to decide. He says: 'You're not a faggot. You can be *gay* ... but you don't have to let nobody call you a faggot'. In this way, Juan frees Chiron from the burden of becoming, just as he frees him from the weight of his body when he holds him in the water. He allows Chiron to simply be, opening the possibility of a queer sexuality without naming or proscribing it as the school bullies, and even Paula, have done.

The three-part structure of the film is not necessarily new, with Jenkins citing *Three Times* as his inspiration, and the three-act play is one of the foundational structures of screenwriting (Field 1979). What makes *Moonlight* unusual in its deployment of this narrative and character tryptic is first, the different appearances of the actors and second, the choice of this form for a coming-of-age narrative. *Moonlight* is one of the only coming-of-age dramas to distinguish between the three stages of the character's life sharply using three different looking and differently aged actors: 'Little' (Hibbert, 12), 'Chiron' (Sanders, 21) and 'Black' (Rhodes, 26). This difference between the actors and characters was sought by Jenkins, who describes an extraordinary filming process in which he steadfastly refused to allow the actors to meet one another or rehearse together, despite the repeated pleas of Rhodes. Rhodes would later describe Jenkins's ability to attain coherence across the three stages of Chiron's life as a kind of 'magic trick' (quoted in Chen 2017). This coherence comes about, as previously described, through the repetition of certain gestures (the lowering of his head and eyes), actions (bathing, for example), and a similar gentle watchfulness, what Jenkins calls a 'vibe and spirituality' (quoted in ibid.). The difference between the actors offers a stark counterpoint to a film like Linklater's *Boyhood*, which achieves a forceful reality effect in its *Bildungsroman*: the film was shot for three or four days a year for 12 years, thus offering a hyper-realistic examination of physical and interpersonal transformations of its central character.

Yet, why did Jenkins go to such lengths to ensure that audiences would perceive Chiron differently at these three stages of his life, while also grasping at something essential that remained consistent in the character? For me, this balancing act is one of the great strengths of the film. It captures the feeling that one can be three quite different people at these stages of life, that the experiences one has can change one profoundly, and yet some threads of character will be pulled across the years. It invites reflection on how one might be altered had certain experiences not occurred and the distillations of character that might have always remained the same, irrespective of external circumstance. Indeed, Jenkins notes, 'I did want the character to be a different person in each chapter, because I felt the world around them is shaping them so much that they've literally become a different person' (quoted in Chen 2017). The factors that shape Chiron as a child and as a teenager are manifold, but boys and girls presented in many other coming-of-age dramas can afford to make mistakes and get things wrong on their journey to adulthood, such as the child in *Boyhood*. No such privilege is afforded to Chiron; if anything, his mistakes seem to be punished excessively, such as being carried off to gaol for fighting back against Terrel the bully by hitting him over the head with a chair. No excuses are made for Chiron – not that he is being bullied or that his mother is an addict. As Coates notes of the harsh punishments meted out to Black children in American schools, 'educated children never offered excuses – certainly not childhood itself. The world had no time for the childhoods of black boys and girls' (2015: 25).

Ian Wojcik-Andrews argues that, in Western cinema, child characters are 'framed by linear narratives' that begin in harmony, followed by 'a disruption […] that propels the child forward on a journey' (2000: xii). Yet, Chiron's journey to adulthood is not depicted as one in which a baseline of stability or peace is broken by a single, defining event, but rather, his childhood and adolescence are narrated as an ebb and flow between safety and danger, moments of joy and instances of pain and sorrow. In so doing, Jenkins captures the messiness of growing up, the ways in which the clear, completed narrative trajectory of so many coming-of-age narratives is in reality incomplete, contingent and may not lead to the 'whole' adult who emerges at the end of the film. Instead, *Moonlight* shows the ways in which the circumstances of a particular life can produce some growth but can also stunt the child who, nonetheless, lingers in the adult.

'Tarell and I are that boy. We are Chiron'. It is noteworthy that Jenkins speaks of their identification with Chiron in the present tense. Importantly, this is a vision of a childhood that is not, as Dumas and Nelson note, in relation to Black boyhoods, 'put aside' (2016: 35). Jenkins shows that childhood remains with adults throughout their lives, and this raises political questions about how society views childhood, particularly in the cases of minority and underprivileged kids: when does a child become an adult with adult responsibility and adult punishment? Section III of the film, which looks at adult Chiron, does not begin with an image of the grown man, but rather with an image of Paula from the perspective of the child Chiron. Paula, framed closely by the hallway of their flat, advances toward the camera with a downturned, contemptuous expression and screams, 'Don't look at me!'. While the viewer does not see an image of Chiron, Paula's downturned gaze and the repetition of this sequence, lets the spectator know that we are watching this maternal anger unfold through Chiron's eyes. The short sequence ends, and the camera cuts to the distressed adult in his bed, now transformed into a 20-something year old man.

McCraney echoes this sense of the frightened child who lives on in the adult when he asks, 'what does it mean to be the child of a crack addict in the world? And what am I carrying around that I'm not necessarily thinking about on the surface level?' (McCraney 2017). The film offers Chiron and Paula some potential for reconciliation in a heartbreaking scene between the pair in the breezy garden of a rehab centre, where an older and sober Paula asks for forgiveness. She tells Chiron, 'your heart ain't gotta be black like mine', implying that the adult has 'blackened' his heart, along with his name, in order to survive. Paula's words here are an exhortation for Chiron to open, to soften and, perhaps, to grow. It is after, and perhaps because of, this conversation with Paula that Chiron makes the journey from Atlanta to Miami to see Kevin (see Bradley 2017). This reunion leads to the film's penultimate image, a medium two shot of Chiron and Kevin embracing, with Chiron's head resting on his friend's shoulder.

Indeed, not only does the adult section of the film begin with the child's point of view, it also ends with an image of Chiron as 'Little'. The scene cuts away from the grown Chiron and Kevin's embrace, using the sound of a sea breeze and a rushing tide as a sound bridge, to an image of the child Chiron looking out over the waves. Thick with blue light, the background of the image is cut in three, the bright blue of the sky, to the darker water and, in the foreground, the white tipped waves as they meet the shore. In the centre stands Chiron as a child, facing out to sea wearing a pair of white shorts with the tips of his shoulder blades catching two dots of bright light. The camera zooms in slowly onto the back of his head and, in a head and shoulders shot, Chiron turns to look directly at the camera, parting his lips slightly and holding the direct gaze of the viewer (Figure 5.3).

According to Stella Bolaki, the *Bildungsroman* has a 'linear and teleological movement, and a closure that avoids openness' (2011: 139). By contrast, the ending of *Moonlight* does not offer a clear sense of conclusion and can be read ambiguously. The final image also has much in common with the closing images of François Truffaut's masterful New Wave coming-of-age drama, *Les 400 Coups* (*The 400 Blows* 1959). In this film, the young protagonist, Antoine Doinel (Jean-Pierre Leaud), has escaped from the reform school where he has been placed and abandoned by his mother. In this closing sequence, Doinel runs toward the sea: it is the first time he has seen it, and he splashes into the waves before realizing that he can run no further. He turns toward the shore, and toward the camera, as it zooms into a freeze frame of his face. His

Figure 5.3 The final image of the film – the child Chiron by the ocean.

expression of uncertainty captures, as Roger Ebert notes, the fact that the boy is 'caught between land and water, between past and future' (1999).

Yet, for all their similarity, the final image in *Moonlight* functions somewhat differently. First, unlike Doinel, who is in flight toward the sea, Chiron stands still, and his turning to the camera is not the retreat of one who is trapped by the water's edge but of one who chooses to look. The expression on his face is less one of uncertainty but, rather, one of possibility. Speaking of the character of Chiron, McCraney has said, 'I am still that vulnerable child' (2017). This final image suggests that an acceptance of the vulnerable child within may open up emotional transformation for the adult. Moreover, the image of child Chiron at the sea serves more as a coda, a repeated refrain, that allows listeners to 'look back', 'take it all in', creating 'a sense of balance' (Burkhart 2005: 12). We have already seen Chiron as an adult, so this final image serves not as the conclusion of his cinematic and coming-of-age journey but, rather, as a memory, vision or dream of what has gone before. It underscores, again, that the child in Chiron lives on in the adult, suggesting that perhaps this moment of tenderness with Kevin can allow that child, who once found freedom at the sea, to find that freedom again. Thus, by framing Section III of the film, Chiron's adulthood, by two sets of images from the perspective of the child, Jenkins invites the viewer to consider the ways in which we all encompass the child we once were.

Conclusion

Bazin argues that some films about childhood treat it 'as if it were open to our understanding and empathy', because they rely on 'our sympathy for children who manifest feelings that are comprehensible to us' (1997: 123). By providing viewers with moments of tender access to Chiron's private and intimate life from childhood through to adolescence and early adulthood, Jenkins makes Chiron not only visible but comprehensible. That a Black child would not be comprehensible, or even seen as a child, is a symptom of the disturbing racist legacy of image-making. *Moonlight* stands as a reminder that we were all once vulnerable children dependent on the care and empathy of others and that, in the troubling climate of the present in which systemic racial prejudice and bigotry haunt the political scene, some children remain much more vulnerable than others.

6 Epilogue

Love and *Moonlight*

As I was completing the final edits on this manuscript, I found myself stumbling on many sentences with the correlative conjunction, 'both/and'. I then recalled a quote from critic Michael Dyson about *Boyz N the Hood* in which he says that director Singleton refuses to construct a nature and nurture dichotomy, instead offering 'an Afrocentric world of both/and' (1992: 126). This statement also summons Guerrero's writing on African American music in film and the false dichotomy white directors create between hip-hop ('low culture') and gospel ('high culture'); he notes that, 'black sensibility by far transcends such stiff dualisms, for its aim is to express integration and the continuity of black life' (1993: 51). Such refusals of strict categorization and the occupation of multiple subject positions and artistic traditions speak to the work of Marlon Riggs, who melded documentary and poetry and music and testimony in his work. Wallenberg argues that Riggs's work, and that of his contemporary Isaac Julien, should be viewed, 'not in terms of an either/or, but in terms of an inclusive *and*' because of the ways these artists demonstrate that 'black queerness, or queer blackness, cannot be divided' (2004: 129).

Moonlight is the epitome of a work that refuses to be tied definitively into a particular category to the exclusion of other attributes. Created at the end of a momentous African American presidency and the beginning of an inauguration that was bound up in fantasies of white America, the film also straddled a moment in Hollywood when the lack of minority representation was being virulently critiqued and a wave of Black talent was sweeping the industry. *Moonlight* also evokes some familiar cinematic stereotypes of Black men and women on film but disrupts them and, thus, offers both familiarity and distinctiveness in its presentation of Chiron, Juan, Kevin and Paula. The film, furthermore, invites a questioning of the categories of queer versus LGBT-themed cinema, but within this debate, the work of E. Patrick Johnson points instead to a third term: quare. This reconfiguration

DOI: 10.4324/9780429055294-6

accounts for Chiron's sexuality in complex ways that acknowledge the significance of race and class to his identity as well.

The style of *Moonlight* perhaps most clearly captures the film's refusal of exclusive classifications: a film that draws on both arthouse traditions and Black independent filmmaking, the narrative of *Moonlight* further combines linear and cyclical storytelling. Moreover, just as Jenkins renders the streets of Liberty City iridescent through light, cinematography and colour, setting up what might appear like a contradiction between traditional conceptions of aesthetic beauty and painful social-realist content, so too he disturbs elitist perceptions of 'high' and 'low' culture in terms of music. The last chapter of this book sought to address another dichotomy: the tension in the press and popular reception of *Moonlight* between its appeal to mass audiences and its evocation of very specific lives and circumstances. However, the cinematic and social appeal of childhood is evoked by Jenkins in his vision of a complex, joyful, sorrowful and playful Black boyhood; *Moonlight* refuses to 'put aside' Chiron's childhood, instead showing how it lives on in the man he becomes.

For many viewers, *Moonlight* is an easy film to love and not only because of the rich colours, slick cinematography and reverberant soundscape. Indeed, in my own writing of this book over the course of several years, *Moonlight* continued to move me, offering up fresh insights with every rewatching, every reading undertaken, and each new class discussion. This may, in part, be due to the film's openness to the multiple and intersecting identities, stories and styles outlined above. It opens, rather than closes, interpretation at every turn, inviting emotion as much as it invites interpretation. *Moonlight* is about love: the love of parents and surrogate parents, willingly bestowed love, love twisted by addiction, tentative love, sensual love, squashed love, love that turns to violence, love lost and love rediscovered. It is about romantic love and friendship love and the entanglements of each; it tackles the joys of love and the sorrow of neglect at the hands of parents and carers. In this multifaceted vision, *Moonlight* recalls James Baldwin's words: 'Love does not begin and end the way we seem to think it does. Love is a battle. Love is a war. Love is growing up' (1998: 220). Love is not easy, but it is nothing less than 'the story of a lifetime' – the passage to adulthood. *Moonlight* captures the complexity of love: it is both pleasure and pain, absence and presence, and it ebbs and flows like a tide, shaping and moulding the landscape of a life.

Bibliography

Aaron, M. (2004) 'New Queer Cinema: An Introduction', in Michele Aaron (ed) *New Queer Cinema: A Critical Reader*, Edinburgh: Edinburgh University Press, pp. 3–14.

Adams, T. (2017) '*Moonlight*'s Writer Tarell Alvin McCraney: "The Story Needed to Be Out There"', *Observer*, online, 5 February, https://www.theguardian.com/film/2017/feb/05/moonlight-writer-tarell-alvin-mccraney-observer-interview.

Ahmed, S. (2006) *Queer Phenomenology: Orientations, Objects, Others*, Durham, NC: Duke University Press.

Ahmed, S. (2014) *The Cultural Politics of Emotion*, 2nd edition, Edinburgh: Edinburgh University Press.

Allen, B. (2017) 'Slow Movies', *Hudson Review* (Winter), pp. 624–30.

Als, H. (2016) '"Moonlight" Undoes Our Expectations', *New York Times*, online, 17 October, https://www.newyorker.com/magazine/2016/10/24/moonlight-undoes-our-expectations.

Amossy, R. (1982) 'The Cliché in the Reading Process', *SubStance*, Vol. 11, No. 4, pp. 34–45 (translated by Terese Lyons).

Anderson, J. (2016) '"Moonlight" Review: Searing, Splendid Night Vision', *Wall Street Journal*, online, 21 October, https://www.wsj.com/articles/moonlight-review-searing-splendid-night-vision-1476988100.

Anderson-Moore, O. (2018) 'Oscar-Winner Barry Jenkins: "People Told Me *Moonlight* Would Be Career Suicide"', *No Film School*, online, 12 March, https://nofilmschool.com/2018/03/barry-jenkins-sxsw-2018-film-keynote.

Anon. (2009) 'Dissecting the 2008 Electorate: Most Diverse in U.S. History', *Pew Research Center*, online, 30 April, https://www.pewresearch.org/hispanic/2009/04/30/dissecting-the-2008-electorate-most-diverse-in-us-history/#about-this-report.

Anon. (2016) 'Moonlight, Film Review: A Form of Poetry, at Once Utterly Specific and Universal', *Evening Standard*, online, [no date], https://www.standard.co.uk/go/london/film/moonlight-film-review-a-form-of-poetry-at-once-utterly-specific-and-universal-a3680041.html.

Anon. (2021a) 'Moonlight', *Box Office Mojo*, online, 12 April, https://www.imdb.com/title/tt4975722/.

Anon. (2021b) 'Moonlight', *Internet Movie Database (IMDb)*, online, 12 April, https://www.imdb.com/title/tt4975722/.

Ariès, P. (1962) *Centuries of Childhood: A Social History of Family Life*, Toronto: Jonathan Cape.

Arroyo, J. (1993) 'Death, Desire and Identity: The Political Unconscious of "New Queer Cinema"', in J. Bristow and A.R. Wilson (eds) *Activating Theory: Lesbian, Gay, Bisexual Politics*, London: Lawrence and Wishart, pp. 72–98.

Baldwin, J. (1968) 'Sidney Poitier', *Look*, Vol. 23 (July), p. 56.

Baldwin, J. (1998) 'In Search of a Majority', in Toni Morrison (ed) *James Baldwin: Collected Essays*, New York: Library of America, pp. 215–21.

Baldwin, J. (2014) *James Baldwin: The Last Interview: And Other Conversations*, New York: Melville House Publishing.

Barfield, T. (2017) 'In *Moonlight*', *LA Review of Books*, online, 3 March, https://marginalia.lareviewofbooks.org/in-moonlight/.

Baron, Z. (2017) 'How A24 is Disrupting Hollywood', *GQ*, online, 9 May, https://www.gq.com/story/a24-studio-oral-history.

Bastién, A.J. (2017) 'The Empathy Machine: Why Moonlight Isn't Universal and That's a Good Thing', *Cleo: A Journal of Film and Television*, Vol. 5, No. 1, http://cleojournal.com/2017/04/21/empathy-machine-moonlight-isnt-universal-thats-good-thing/.

Bausch, K. (2013) 'Superflies into Superkillers: Black Masculinity from Blaxploitation to New Black Realism', *Journal of Popular Culture*, Vol. 46, No. 2, pp. 257–76.

Bazin, A. (1997) 'Review of *Germany, Ground Zero*', in B. Cardullo (ed) *Bazin at Work: Major Essays and Reviews From the Forties and Fifties*, New York: Routledge, pp. 121–4.

Beirich, H. and Schlatter, E. (2014) 'Backlash: Racism and the Presidency of Barack Obama', in M. Ledwidge, K. Verney, and I. Parmar (eds) *Barack Obama and the Myth of a Post-Racial America*, London: Routledge, pp. 80–101.

Benshoff, H.M. and Griffin, S. (2004) 'General Introduction' in H. Benshoff, and S. Griffin (eds) *Queer Cinema: The Film Reader*, London: Routledge, pp. 1–15.

Berger, J. (1973) *Ways of Seeing*, Penguin: London.

Bernstein, R. (2011) *Racial Innocence: Performing African American Childhood from Slavery to Civil Rights*, New York: New York University Press.

Bhabha, H.K. (2009) *The Location of Culture*, London: Routledge.

Blackwell, B. (2019) 'Cleveland Police Officer Shot Tamir Rice Immediately After Leaving Moving Patrol Car', *Cleaveland.com*, online, 12 January, https://www.cleveland.com/metro/2014/11/cleveland_police_officer_shot_1.html (originally published in 2014).

Bogle, D. (1994) *Toms, Coons, Mulattoes, Mammies, & Bucks: An Interpretive History of Blacks in American Films*, Brighton: Roundhouse.

Bolaki, S. (2012) *Unsettling the Bildungsroman: Reading Contemporary Ethnic Women's Fiction*, Amsterdam: Rodopi.

Bordwell, D. (1985) *Narration in Fiction Film*, Madison, WI: University of Wisconsin Press.

Boyce Gillespie, M. (2017) 'One Step Ahead: A Conversation with Barry Jenkins', *Film Quarterly*, Vol. 70, No. 3, pp. 52–62.

Boylorn, R. (2016) 'Moonlight Musings & Motherhood: On Paula, Teresa and the Complicated Role of (Bad) Black Mamas in Film', *Crunk Feminist Collective*, online, 28 October, https://www.crunkfeministcollective.com/2016/10/28/moon light-musings-motherhood-on-paula-teresa-and-the-complicated-role-of-bad-bl ack-mamas-in-film.

Bradbury, S. (2019) 'Stephan James on *If Beale Street Could Talk*: 'It's Such a Special Thing for Cinema, the Idea that Black Love Exists', *BFI News*, online, 18 February, https://www2.bfi.org.uk/news-opinion/news-bfi/interviews/ste phan-james-barry-jenkins-if-beale-street-could-talk.

Bradley, R. (2017) 'Vestiges of Motherhood: The Maternal Function in Recent Black Cinema', *Film Quarterly*, Vol. 71, No. 2, pp. 46–52.

Braga, A.A. and Brunson, R.K (2015) 'The Police and Public Discourse on "Black-on-Black" Violence', *New Perspectives in Policing*, May 2015, pp. 1–22.

Brathwaite, L.F. (2017) 'A *Moonlight* Revolution: The Black Queer Experience Comes of Age in America', *Out*, online, 31 January, https://www.out.com/out -exclusives/2017/1/31/moonlight-revolution-black-queer-experience-comes-age -america.

Bruce, L.M.J. (2019) 'Shore, Unsure: Loitering as a Way of Life', *GLQ: A Journal of Lesbian and Gay Studies*, Vol. 25, No. 2, pp. 352–61.

Brueggemann, T. (2017) '"Moonlight" is the Most Frugal Best Picture Ever: See Analysis of the 10 Lowest-Budget Winners of all Time', *IndieWire*, online, 1 March, https://www.indiewire.com/2017/03/moonlight-wins-top-10-lowest -budget-best-picture-winners-oscar-history-1201788405/.

Burkhart, C. (2005) 'The Phrase Rhythm of Chopin's A-flat Major Mazurka, Op. 59, No. 2', in D. Stein (ed) *Engaging Music: Essays in Music Analysis*, New York: Oxford University Press, pp. 3–12.

Butler, J. (1988) 'Performative Acts and Gender Constitution: An Essay in Phenomenology and Feminist Theory', *Theatre Journal*, Vol. 44, pp. 519–31.

Butler, J. (2004) *Precarious Life: The Powers of Mourning and Violence*, London: Verso.

Butler, J. (2006 [1990]) *Gender Trouble*, New York: Routledge.

Caswell, E. (2015) 'Color Film Was Built for White People. Here's What It did to Dark Skin', *Vox*, online, 18 September, https://www.vox.com/2015/9/18/93488 21/photography-race-bias.

Chan, K. (1998) 'The Construction of Black Male Identity in Black Action Films of the Nineties', *Cinema Journal*, Vol. 37, No. 2, pp. 35–48.

Chen, N. (2017) 'How the Making of *Moonlight* Was like a Magic Trick', *Dazed Digital*, online, 17 February, https://www.dazeddigital.com/artsandculture/articl e/34688/1/barry-jenkins-moonlight-film-magic-trick.

Clinton, J. and Roush, C. (2016) 'Poll: Persistent Partisan Divide Over 'Birther' Question', *NBC News*, online, 10 August, https://www.nbcnews.com/politics/20 16-election/poll-persistent-partisan-divide-over-birther-question-n627446.

Coates, T. (2015) *Between the World and Me*, New York: Spiegel and Grau.

Coates, T. (2017a). 'The First White President', *Atlantic*, online, October, https:/
/www.theatlantic.com/magazine/archive/2017/10/the-first-white-president-ta-n
ehisi-coates/537909/.

Coates, T. (2017b). 'We Should Have Seen Trump Coming', *Guardian*, online,
29 September, https://www.theguardian.com/news/2017/sep/29/we-should-
have-seen-trump-coming.

Collier, A. (1989) 'Why Hollywood Ignores Black Love and Intimacy', *Ebony*,
April, pp. 41–4.

Collin, R. (2016) 'Moonlight Review: A Graceful, Compassionate Coming-of-Age
Heartbreaker', *Telegraph*, online, 6 October, https://www.telegraph.co.uk/films
/0/moonlight-review-a-graceful-compassionate-coming-of-age-heartbre/.

Contreras, D.T. (2004) 'New Queer Cinema: Spectacle, Race, Utopia', in M. Aaron
(ed) *New Queer Cinema: A Critical Reader*, Edinburgh: Edinburgh University
Press, pp. 119–28.

Cooper, B. and Pease, E.C. (2008) 'Framing *Brokeback Mountain*: How the
Popular Press Corralled the "Gay Cowboy Movie"', *Critical Studies in Media
Communication*, Vol. 25, No. 3, pp 249–73.

Copeland, K.J. (2017) '*Moonlight*, Directed by Barry Jenkins', *Journal of
Homosexuality*, Vol. 65, No. 5, pp. 687–9.

Cover, R. (2000) 'First Contact: Queer Theory, Sexual Identity, and "Mainstream"
Film', *International Journal of Sexuality and Gender Studies*, Vol. 5, pp. 71–89.

Coyle, J. (2016) '*Moonlight* Stars Reflect on Playing Same Character at Three
Different Ages', *Christian Science Monitor*, online, 30 October, https://www
.csmonitor.com/The-Culture/Movies/2016/1030/Moonlight-stars-reflect-on-pla
ying-same-character-at-three-different-ages.

Crawley, K. and Hirschfield, P. (2018) 'Examining the School-to-Prison Pipeline
Metaphor', *Oxford Research Encyclopedia of Criminology*, online, 25 June, http:
//oxfordre.com/criminology/view/10.1093/acrefore/9780190264079.001.0001/
acrefore-9780190264079-e-346?print=pdf.

Cuby, M. (2017) 'Why *Moonlight*'s Oscars 2017 Win Is So Important For Queer
Black Men', *Teen Vogue*, online, 27 February, https://www.teenvogue.com/story
/why-moonlights-oscars-2017-win-is-so-important-for-queer-black-men.

Cunningham, H. (2006) *Children and Childhood in Western Society Since 1500*,
New York: Longman.

Daniel, R. (2016) 'Should Sociologists Care about #OscarsSoWhite?', *Researching
Sociology*, online, 20 January, http://eprints.lse.ac.uk/82301/.

Danuta Walters, S. (2012) 'The Kids Are All Right But the Lesbians Aren't: Queer
Kinship in US Culture', in *Sexualities*, Vol. 15, No. 8, pp. 917–33.

Dawson, M.C. and Bobo, L.D. (2009) 'One Year Later and the Myth of a post-Racial
Society', *Du Bois Review: Social Science Research on Race*, Vol. 6, No. 2, pp. 247–9.

Del Barco, M. (2016) 'In "Moonlight", Growing Up Black, Gay And Poor In 1980s
Miami', *NPR*, online, 18 October, https://www.npr.org/2016/10/18/498358778/
moonlight-coming-of-age-in-miami-during-the-war-on-drugs-era.

DeMause, L. (1974) *The History of Childhood: Untold Story of Child Abuse*, New
York: Jason Aronson.

Devega, C. (2016) '"Moonlight" and "Loving": Film as Symbolic Resistance in the Age of Trump', *Salon*, online, 11 December, https://www.salon.com/2016/12/10/moonlight-and-loving-film-as-symbolic-resistance-in-the-age-of-trump/.

Devere Brody, J. (2007) 'Boyz Do Cry: Screening Histories White Lies', in J. Stacey and S. Street (eds) *Queer Screen: A Screen Reader*, Oxford: Routledge, pp. 289–95.

Diawara, M. (1993) 'Black American Cinema: The New Realism', in M. Diawara (ed) *Black American Cinema*, London: Routledge, pp. 3–25.

Dietz, J. (2019) 'Best Movies of the Decade (2010–19)', *Metacritic*, online, 18 November, https://www.metacritic.com/feature/best-movies-of-the-decade-2010s.

Doane, M.A. (1999) 'Film and the Masquerade: Theorizing the Female Spectator', in S. Thornham (ed) *Feminist Film Theory: A Reader*, Edinburgh: Edinburgh University Press, pp. 418–36.

Doty, A. (1998) 'Queer Theory', in J. Hill and P. Church Gibson (eds) *The Oxford Guide to Film Studies*, Oxford: Oxford University Press, pp. 148–52.

Drake, S.C. (2016) 'A Meditation on the Soundscapes of Black Boyhood and Disruptive Imaginations', *Souls*, Vol. 18, Nos. 2–4, pp. 446–58.

Dumas, M.J. and Nelson, J.D. (2016) '(Re)Imagining Black Boyhood: Toward a Critical Framework for Educational Research', *Harvard Educational Review*, Vol. 86, No. 1, pp. 27–47.

Dyer, R. (1982) 'Don't Look Now', *Screen*, Vol. 23, Nos. 3–4, pp. 61–73.

Dyer, R. (1997) *White: Essays on Race and Culture*, London: Routledge.

Dyson, M.E. (1992) 'Between Apocalypse and Redemption: John Singleton's "Boyz N the Hood"', *Cultural Critique*, Vol. 21, pp. 121–41.

Ebert, R. (1999) 'The 400 Blows', *RogerEbert.com*, online, 8 August, https://www.rogerebert.com/reviews/great-movie-the-400-blows-1959.

Ebert, R. (2018) 'Video: Roger Ebert on Empathy', *RogerEbert.com*, online, 4 April, https://www.rogerebert.com/empathy/video-roger-ebert-on-empathy (originally published in 2013).

Edelman, L. (2004) *No Future: Queer Theory and the Death Drive*, Durham, NC: Duke University Press.

Feagin, S.L. (1998) 'The Pleasures of Tragedy', in S. Feagin and P. Maynard (eds) *Aesthetics*, Oxford: Oxford University Press, pp. 305–13.

Field, S. (1979) *Screenplay: The Foundations of Screenwriting*, New York: Dell Publishing Company.

Fisher, L. (2017) 'How "Moonlight" Became the Little Film that Could and Made It to the Oscars', *ABC News*, online, 22 February, https://abcnews.go.com/Entertainment/moonlight-film-made-oscars/story?id=45328120.

Flory, D. (2019) 'Moonlight, Film Noir, and Melodrama', *Western Journal of Black Studies*, Vol. 43, Nos. 3/4, pp. 104–13.

Foster, J.D. (2019) 'Tricks of the (Colorblind) Trade: Hollywood's Preservation of White Supremacy in the Age of Obama', in S.E. Turner and S. Nilsen (eds) *The Myth of Colorblindness: Race and Ethnicity in American Cinema*, London: Palgrave Macmillan, pp. 173–91.

Fragoso, S. (2016) '"Moonlight" Review: Barry Jenkins Tracks a Tragic Childhood in Powerful Film', *Wrap*, online, 20 October, https://www.thewrap.com/moonli ght-review-2016/.

Fritz, B. (2016) '2016 Turning Out to Be the Year of the Hollywood Flop', *Market Watch/Wall Street Journal*, online, 15 August, https://www.marketwatch.com/st ory/2016-turning-out-to-be-the-year-of-the-hollywood-flop-2016-08-14.

Gates, R. (2017) 'The Last Shall be First: Aesthetics and Politics in Black Film and Media', *Film Quarterly*, Vol. 71, No. 2, pp. 38–45.

Gates, R. and Boyce Gillespie, M. (2019) 'Reclaiming Black Film and Media Studies', *Film Quarterly*, Vol. 72, No. 3, pp. 13–15.

Gay, R. (2017) *Hunger: A Memoir of (My) Body*, London: Harper Collins.

Goldstein, N. (2011) 'Barack Obama's Real Record on LGBT Rights', *Guardian*, online, 23 June, https://www.theguardian.com/commentisfree/cifamerica/2011/ jun/23/gay-rights-barack-obama.

Gray, B. (2017) '*Call Me By Your Name, Moonlight*, and the Cost of Critical Success for Queer Films', *Slate*, online, 21 November, https://slate.com/human-interest/2017/11 /call-me-by-your-names-lack-of-explicit-sex-may-explain-its-critical-success.html.

Greven, D. (2018) 'Unlovely Spectacle: D.A. Miller on *Call Me By Your Name*', *Film International*, online, 30 March, http://filmint.nu/?p=23937.

Guerrero, E. (1993) *Framing Blackness: The African American Image in Film*, Philadelphia, PA: Temple University Press.

Halberstam, J. (2018) *Trans*: A Quick and Quirky Account of Gender Variability*, Oakland, CA: University of California Press.

Halberstam, J. (2000) 'Telling Tales: Brandon Teena, Billy Tipton, and Transgender Biography', *Auto/Biography Studies*, Vol. 15, No. 1, pp. 62–81.

Hale, C. (2014) 'Different Placements of Spirit: African American Musicians Historicizing in Sound', Doctoral Dissertation submitted to City University of New York, pp. 1–149.

Hannah-Jones, N. (2017) 'From Bittersweet Childhoods to "Moonlight"', *New York Times*, online, 4 January, https://www.nytimes.com/2017/01/04/movies/moo nlight-barry-jenkins-tarell-alvin-mccraney-interview.html.

Hans, S. (2018) '*Moonlight* First-look Review: Masculinity, Differently', *Sight and Sound*, online, 8 February, https://www2.bfi.org.uk/news-opinion/sight-sound-m agazine/reviews-recommendations/moonlight-first-look.

Hayward, S. (2000) *Cinema Studies: The Key Concepts*, 2nd edition, London: Routledge.

Hill Collins, P. (2005) *Black Sexual Politics: African Americans, Gender, and the New Racism*, Oxford: Routledge.

Hirway, H. (2017) 'How *Moonlight*'s Composer Chopped and Screwed Classical Music', *Vulture*, online, 1 February, https://www.vulture.com/2017/02/song-exp loder-inside-moonlights-score.html.

Hochschild, A. (2016) *Strangers in their Own Land: Anger and Mourning on the American Right*, New York: The New Press.

Hooks, B. (2015) *Black Looks: Race and Representation*, 2nd edition, London: Routledge.

Hornaday, A. (2017) '"Moonlight" Is Both a Tough Coming-of-Age Tale and a Tender Testament to Love', *Washington Post*, online, 27 October, https://ww w.washingtonpost.com/goingoutguide/movies/moonlight-is-both-a-tough-co ming-of-age-tale-and-a-tender-testament-to-love/2016/10/27/45d88eea-9b80-11 e6-9980-50913d68eacb_story.html.

Hughey, M.W. (2011) 'Measuring Racial Progress in America: The Tangled Path', in G.S. Parks, and M.W. Hughey (eds) *The Obamas and a (Post) Racial America?*, Oxford: Oxford University Press, pp. 1–24.

Jackson, R. (2006) *Scripting the Black Masculine Body*, Albany: State University of New York Press.

Jagose, A. (1997) *Queer Theory: An Introduction*, New York: New York University Press.

Johnson, E.P. (2001) '"Quare" Studies, or (Almost) Everything I Know About Queer Studies I Learned from My Grandmother', *Text and Performance Quarterly*, Vol. 21, No. 1, pp. 1–25.

Johnson, E.P. (2003) 'The Specter of the Black Fag', *Journal of Homosexuality*, Vol. 45, No. 2, pp. 217–34.

Johnson, E.P (2019) 'In the Quare Light of the Moon: Poverty, Sexuality and Makeshift Masculinity in *Moonlight*', *Western Journal of Black Studies*, Vol. 43, Nos. 3–4, pp. 70–80.

Jones, J. (1991) 'The New Ghetto Aesthetic', *Wide Angle*, Vol. 13, Nos. 3–4, pp. 32–44.

Jones, J. (1993) 'The Construction of Black Sexuality' in M. Diawara (ed) *Black American Cinema*, London: Routledge, pp. 247–56.

Jones, J. (2019) 'Moonlight Riff: Examining Rifts between *Presentations* of Black, Gay, Male Humanity and *Representations* of Black, Gay, Male Non-Humanity in *Moonlight*', *Western Journal of Black Studies*, Vol. 43, Nos. 3–4, pp. 90–103.

Jung, E.A. (2018) 'What's Happening to 'Queer' Cinema in the LGBT Film Boom?', *Vulture*, online, 16 May, https://www.vulture.com/2018/05/queer-cinema-whats -happening-to-it.html.

Kannan, M., Hall, R. and Hughey, M.W. (2017) 'Watching *Moonlight* in the Twilight of Obama', *Humanity & Society*, Vol. 41, No. 3, pp. 287–98.

Kennedy, T.M. (2014) 'Sustaining White Homonormativity: *The Kids Are All Right* as Public Pedagogy', *Journal of Lesbian Studies*, Vol. 18, No. 2, pp. 118–32.

Kermode, M. (2017) 'Moonlight Review: A Five-Star Symphony of Love', *Guardian*, online, 19 February, https://www.theguardian.com/film/2017/feb/19/ moonlight-review-five-star.

Kilday, G. (2016) 'How 'Moonlight' Became a "Personal Memoir" for Director Barry Jenkins', *Hollywood Reporter*, online, 11 November, https://www.hol lywoodreporter.com/features/how-moonlight-became-a-personal-memoir-dir ector-barry-jenkins-i-knew-story-like-back-my-han.

Kingstone S. (2012) 'Obama's Gay Marriage Backing Gamble', *BBC News*, online, 10 May, https://www.bbc.co.uk/news/av/world-us-canada-18015513.

Kukar, P. (2016) '"The Very Unrecognizability of the Other": The Pedagogical Challenge of Empathy', *Philosophical Inquiry in Education*, Vol. 24, No. 1, pp. 1–14.

Lang, B. (2018) 'Apple Taps A24 to Produce Slate of Films', *Variety*, online, 15 November, https://variety.com/2018/film/news/apple-a24-films-1203 029800/.

Latif, N. (2017) 'It's lit! How Film Finally Learned to Light Black Skin', *Guardian*, online, 18 September, https://www.theguardian.com/film/2017/sep/21/its-lit-ho w-film-finally-learned-how-to-light-black-skin.

LeBeau, V. (2008) *Childhood and Cinema*, London: Reaktion Books.

Lee, A. (2017a) 'Why Luca Guadagnino Didn't Include Gay Actors or Explicit Sex Scenes in 'Call Me by Your Name' (Q&A)', *The Hollywood Reporter*, online, 2 August, https://www.hollywoodreporter.com/news/call-me-by-your-name- why-luca-guadagnino-left-gay-actors-explicit-sex-scenes-q-a-973256.

Lee, B. (2016) 'Interview: Moonlight's Tarell Alvin McCraney: 'I never Had a Coming Out Moment'', *Guardian*, online, 21 October, https://www.theguardian .com/film/2016/oct/21/moonlight-film-tarell-alvin-mccraney-interview.

Lee, B. (2017) 'Why *Moonlight* should Win the Best Picture Oscar', *Guardian*, online, 20 February, https://www.theguardian.com/film/2017/feb/20/why-m oonlight-should-win-the-best-picture-oscar.

Lee, J. (2017) '*Moonlight* Isn't All about Sex: and It's All the More Queer for It', *Little White Lies*, online, 11 February, https://lwlies.com/articles/moonlight-ba rry-jenkins-sex-queer-cinema/.

Lodge, G. (2017a) 'After the Moonlight Fades: What's Next for LGBT Cinema', *Guardian*, online, 7 February, theguardian.com/film/2017/mar/07/moonlight-fu ture-lgbt-movies.

Lodge, G. (2017b) 'Does Moonlight Show Gay Cinema Has to be Sexless to Succeed?', *Guardian*, online, 5 January, https://www.theguardian.com/film /2017/jan/05/does-moonlight-prove-that-gay-cinema-has-to-be-sexless-to -succeed.

Loist, S. (2017) 'Crossover Dreams: Global Circulation of Queer Film on the Film Festival Circuits', *Diogenes*, Vol. 62, No. 1, pp. 57–72.

Long, C. (2017), 'Film Review: *Moonlight* and *Hidden Figures*', *Times*, online, 19 February, https://www.thetimes.co.uk/article/film-review-moonlight-and -hidden-figures-fxj5rf7qq.

Loreck, J. (2018) 'Race and Stardom in *Ghost in the Shell*', in *Science Fiction Film and Television*, Vol. 11, No. 1, pp. 37–44.

Lury, K. (2005) 'The Child in Film and Television: Introduction', *Screen*, Vol. 46, No. 3, pp. 307–14.

Lury, K. (2018) 'Children, Objects and Motion... Balloons, Bikes, Kites and Tethered Flight', in Conference Paper at Retrenching/*Entrenching* Youth: *Mobility and Stasis in* Youth Culture Representations *on* Screen, University of Liverpool, 4 and 5 June 2018.

Marks, L. (2000) *The Skin of the Film*, Durham and London: Duke University Press.

McCraney, T.A. (2017) '"I'm Still that Vulnerable Boy"', *Newsnight* [video], online, 16 February, https://www.bbc.co.uk/programmes/p04t3zbq.

McDonald, S.N. (2016) 'Barry Jenkin's "Moonlight" and the Gift of Specificity', *The Undefeated*, online, 28 October, https://theundefeated.com/features/director-barry-jenkins-moonlight-movie-film-mahershala-ali/.

Meier, A. and Rudwick, E. (1976) *From Plantation to Ghetto*, New York: Hill and Wang.

Mendelson, S. (2015) 'Why Ava DuVernay's "Selma" Oscar Snub Matters', *Forbes*, online, 15 January, https://www.forbes.com/sites/scottmendelson/2015/01/15/why-ava-duvernays-selma-oscar-snub-matters/.

Mendick, H., Allen, K., Ahmad, A and Harvey, L. (2018) *Celebrity, Aspiration, and Contemporary Youth: Education and Equality in an Era of Austerity*, London: Bloomsbury Academic.

Merry, S. (2016) 'How "Moonlight" Became One of the Year's Best Movies', *Washington Post*, online, 28 October, https://www.washingtonpost.com/lifestyle/style/moonlight-is-about-a-poor-black-gay-teen-but-heres-why-it-relates-to-everyone/2016/10/27/01dcca6c-9b7b-11e6-9980-50913d68eacb_story.html.

Miller, D.A. (2007) 'On the Universality of *Brokeback*', *Film Quarterly*, Vol. 60, No. 3, pp. 50–60.

Miller, D.A. (2018) 'Elio's Education', *Los Angeles Review of Books*, online, 19 February, https://lareviewofbooks.org/article/elios-education/.

Molina-Guzmán, I. (2016) '#OscarsSoWhite': How Stuart Hall Explains why Nothing Changes in Hollywood and Everything Is Changing', *Critical Studies in Media Communication*, Vol. 33, No. 5, pp. 438–54.

Morris, S.G. (2020) 'Empathy and the Liberal-Conservative Political Divide in the U.S.', *Journal of Social and Political Psychology*, Vol. 8, No. 1, pp. 8–24.

Myers, S. (2016) 'Why "Moonlight" Relates to Everyone', *Concord Monitor*, online, 1 November, https://www.concordmonitor.com/Why--Moonlight--relates-to-everyone-5752035.

Needham, G. (2010) *Brokeback Mountain*, Edinburgh: Edinburgh University Press.

Nicholson, A. (2016) 'The Aching Beauty of *Moonlight*', *MTV News*, online, 21 October, http://www.mtv.com/news/2946031/moonlight-barry-jenkins-review/.

Norelli, C.N. (2017) 'Scores on Screen. What a Little *Moonlight* Can Do', *Mubi Notebook Column*, online, 14 March, https://mubi.com/notebook/posts/what-a-little-moonlight-can-do.

Obama, B. (2006) *The Audacity of Hope: Thoughts on Reclaiming the American Dream*, London: Crown.

Obama, B. (2007) 'Obama's November 7, 2007, Speech on the "American Dream"', *CNN Politics*, online, 7 November, https://edition.cnn.com/2007/POLITICS/12/21/obama.trans.americandream.

Obama, B. (2009) 'Barack Obama's Back-to-School Speech: Text', *Telegraph*, online, 8 September, https://www.telegraph.co.uk/news/worldnews/barackobama/6154114/Barack-Obamas-back-to-school-speech-text.html.

Obama, B. (2013) 'President Obama on Inequality (transcript)', *Politico*, online, 12 April, https://www.politico.com/story/2013/12/obama-income-inequality-100662.

O'Hara, M.E. (2017) '"Moonlight" Makes Oscars History as 1st LGBTQ Best Picture Winner', *NBC News*, online, 27 February, https://www.nbcnews.com/f

eature/nbc-out/moonlight-makes-oscars-history-1st-lgbtq-best-picture-winner
-n726116.

Olson, D. (2017) *Black Children in Hollywood Cinema: Cast in Shadow*, London: Palgrave Macmillan.

Olson, D. (2018) 'Introduction', in D. Olson (ed) *The Child in World Cinema: Children and Youth in Popular Culture*, New York: Lexington Books, pp. ix–xvii.

Otero, S. and Falola, T. (2013) *Yemoja: Gender, Sexuality, and Creativity in the Latina/o and Afro-Atlantic Diasporas*, Albany, NY: State University of New York Press.

Pallotta, F. (2018) 'The Acceptance Speech the Director of "Moonlight" Never Got to Give', *CNN News*, online, 11 March, https://edition.cnn.com/2018/03/11/enter tainment/barry-jenkins-moonlight-oscar/index.html.

Parmar, P. (1993) 'A Response to B. Ruby Rich', in P. Cook and P. Dodd (eds) *Women and Film: A Sight and Sound Reader*, Philadelphia, PA: Temple University Press, pp. 174–5.

Parris, A. (2016) 'Masculinity and "Moonlight": Eight Black Men Dissect Barry Jenkins' Momentous Film', *CBC News*, online, 4 November, https://www.cbc .ca/arts/masculinity-and-moonlight-eight-black-men-dissect-barry-jenkins-mo mentous-film-1.3836460.

Peacock, S. (2010) *Colour*, Manchester: Manchester University Press.

Pedersen, C. (2014) 'Barack Obama and the Myth of a Post-Racial America', in M. Ledwidge, K. Verney, and I. Parmar (eds) *Barack Obama and the Myth of a Post-Racial America*, London: Routledge, pp. 80–101.

Pick, A. (2004) 'New Queer Cinema and Lesbian Films', in M. Aaron (ed) *New Queer Cinema: A Critical Reader*, Edinburgh: Edinburgh University Press, pp. 103–18.

Poole, G. (1999) *Reel Meals, Set Meals: Food in Film and Theatre*, Sydney: Currency Press.

Powrie, P. (2005) 'Unfamiliar Places: 'Heterospection' and Recent French Films on Children', *Screen*, Vol. 46, No. 3, pp. 341–52.

Pratt, M.L. (2008) *Imperial Eyes: Writing and Transculturation*, 2nd edition, New York: Routledge.

Pulver, A. (2017) 'Moonlight Becomes Him: Barry Jenkins's Journey from a Miami Housing Project to the Oscars', *Guardian*, online, 7 February, https://www.the guardian.com/film/2017/feb/07/moonlight-barry-jenkins-director-interview.

Quashie, K. (2012) *The Sovereignty of Quiet: Beyond Resistance in Black Culture*, New Brunswick, NJ: Rutgers University Press.

Rapold, N. (2016) 'Interview with Barry Jenkins', *Film Comment*, September-October, p. 43.

Reznik, A. (2019) 'Music, Pain, and Healing in Moonlight', *Western Journal of Black Studies*, Vol. 43, Nos. 3–4, pp. 114–21.

Rich, B.R. (2004) 'New Queer Cinema', in M. Aaron (ed) *New Queer Cinema: A Critical Reader*, Edinburgh: Edinburgh University Press, pp. 15–22.

Richeson, J.A. and Bean, M.G. (2011) 'Does Black and Male Still = Threat in the Age of Obama?', in G.S. Parks and M.W. Hughey (eds) *The Obamas and a (Post) Racial America?*, Oxford: Oxford University Press, pp. 94–109.

Riggs, M.T. (1991) 'Black Macho Revisited: Reflections of a Snap! Queen', *Black American Literature Forum*, Vol. 25, No. 2, pp. 389–94.

Roark, D. (2017) '"Moonlight" Is a Flawed, But Rewarding Exercise in Christian Empathy', *Christianity Today*, online, 24 February, https://www.christianityt oday.com/ct/2017/february-web-only/why-church-needs-moonlight.html.

Robehmed, N. (2016) 'Hollywood's Biggest Turkeys Of 2016: The Films That Flopped', *Forbes*, online, 22 November, https://www.forbes.com/sites/natali erobehmed/2016/11/22/hollywoods-biggest-turkeys-of-2016-the-films-that-flop ped/.

Roberts, J.W. (1989) *From Trickster to Badman: The Black Folk Hero in Slavery and Freedom*, Philadelphia, PA: University of Pennsylvania Press.

Robinson, T. (2017) '*Moonlight* Is a Beautifully Nuanced Gay Coming-of-Age Tale', *Verge*, online, 8 January, https://www.theverge.com/2016/9/15/12928752/ moonlight-movie-review-barry-jenkins-tiff-2016.

Rose, S. (2016) 'Black Films Matter: How African American Cinema Fought Back Against Hollywood', *Guardian*, online, 13 October, https://www.theguardian.c om/film/2016/oct/13/do-the-right-thing-how-black-cinema-rose-again.

Roth, L. (2009) 'Looking at Shirley, the Ultimate Norm: Colour Balance, Image Technologies, and Cognitive Equity', *Canadian Journal of Communication*, Vol. 34, No. 1, pp. 111–36.

Roy, S. (2016) 'Slumdog Millionaire: Capitalism, A Love Story', *Journal of Popular Culture*, Vol. 41, No. 1, pp. 155–73.

Ruby, J. (2017) 'Donald Trump Election Made *Moonlight* a must-see Film, says Barry Jenkins', *Evening Standard*, online, 15 February, https://www.standard.co .uk/showbiz/celebrity-news/donald-trump-election-made-moonlight-a-mustsee -film-says-barry-jenkins-a3467361.html.

Russell, F. (2016) 'An Education: On Barry Jenkins's "Moonlight"', *Los Angeles Review of Books*, online, 14 November, https://lareviewofbooks.org/article/educ ation-barry-jenkins-moonlight/.

Ryan, J. (2016) '"This Was a Whitelash": Van Jones' Take on the Election Results', *CNN*, online, 9 November, https://edition.cnn.com/2016/11/09/politics/van-jo nes-results-disappointment-cnntv/index.html.

Schorr, D. (2008) 'A New, 'Post-Racial' Political Era in America', *NPR*, online, 28 January, https://www.npr.org/templates/story/story.php?storyId=18489466.

Scott, A.O. (2016a) 'Barry Jenkins on "Moonlight," a Tale of Black America and Personal Adversity', *New York Times*, online, 6 September, https://www.nytimes. com/2016/09/07/movies/barry-jenkins-interview-moonlight.html.

Scott, A.O. (2016b) '"Moonlight': Is This the Year's Best Movie?', *New York Times*, online, 20 October, https://www.nytimes.com/2016/10/21/movies/moonlight -review.html.

Sexton, J. (2017) *Black Masculinity and the Cinema of Policing*, London: Palgrave Macmillan.

Shaffer, C. (2019) 'Cleveland Police Officer Shoots 12-Year-Old Boy Carrying BB Gun', *Cleaveland.com*, online, 12 January, https://www.cleveland.com/ metro/2014/11/cleveland_police_officer_shoot_6.html (originally published in 2014).

Shary, T. (2005) *Teen Movies: American Youth on Screen*, New York: Wallflower Press.

Shaw, A.R. (2020) 'How Goodie Mob's "Cell Therapy" Predicted the Social Effects of a Pandemic', *RollingOut*, online, 16 April, https://rollingout.com/2020/04/16/how-goodie-mobs-cell-therapy-predicted-the-social-effects-of-a-pandemic/.

Shoard, C. (2017) 'Should Critics of *Moonlight* Be Hounded for Having an Opinion?', *Guardian*, online, 22 February, https://www.theguardian.com/commentisfree/2017/feb/22/moonlight-film-critics-moral-high-ground.

Shone, T. (2016) 'The Quiet Beauty of Barry Jenkins's Festival Hit "Moonlight"', *Newsweek*, online, 21 October, https://www.newsweek.com/2016/10/28/barry-jenkins-moonlight-beauty-512140.html.

Simmons, R. (1991) 'Tongue Untied: An Interview with Marlon Riggs', in E. Hemphill (ed) *Brother to Brother: New Writings by Black Gay Men*, Boston: Alyson Publications, pp. 234–48.

Sims, D. (2016) '*Moonlight* Is a Film of Uncommon Grace', Atlantic, online, 26 October, https://www.theatlantic.com/entertainment/archive/2016/10/moonlight-barry-jenkins-review/505409/.

Sinyard, N. (1992) *Children in the Movies*, London: Batsford Books.

Smith, S.L., Choueiti, M. and Pieper, K. (2014) *Gender Inequality in Popular Films, 2007–2013*, Los Angeles, CA: Annenberg School for Communication and Media Diversity and Social Change Initiative.

Smith, S.L., Choueiti, M., and Pieper, K. (2015) *Race and Ethnicity in 600 Popular Films*, Los Angeles, CA: Annenberg School for Communication and Media Diversity and Social Change Initiative.

Smith, S.L., Choueiti, M, and Pieper, K. (2016) *Inclusion & Invisibility? Gender, Media, Diversity and Social Change Initiative*, Los Angeles, CA: Annenberg School for Communication and Media Diversity and Social Change Initiative.

Springer, K. (2007) 'Divas, Evil Black Bitches, and Bitter Black Women: African American Women in Postfeminist and Post-Civil-Rights Popular Culture', in Y. Tasker and D. Negra (eds) *Interrogating Postfeminism: Gender and the Politics of Popular Culture*, Durham, NC: Duke University Press, pp. 249–76.

Stableford, D. (2012) 'Newsweek Cover: Obama "First Gay President"', *ABC News*, online, 13 May, https://abcnews.go.com/Politics/OTUS/newsweek-cover-obama-gay-president/story?id=16338110.

Stacey, J. and Street, S. (2007) 'Introduction: Queering Screen', in J. Stacey and S. Street (eds) *Queer Screen: A Screen Reader*, Oxford: Routledge, pp. 1–18.

Stallings, L.H. (2019) 'Am I a Faggot?', *GLQ: A Journal of Lesbian and Gay Studies*, Vol. 25, No. 2, pp. 342–51.

Strochlic, N. (2020) 'One in Six Americans could Go Hungry in 2020 as Pandemic Persists', *National Geographic*, online, 24 November, https://www.nationalgeographic.com/history/2020/11/one-in-six-could-go-hungry-2020-as-covid-19-persists/.

Sullivan, J.M. and Johnson, M.S. (2008) 'Race Is on My Mind: Explaining Black Voter's Political Attraction to Barack Obama', *Race, Gender & Class*, Vol. 15, Nos. 3–4, pp. 51–4.

Svetkey, B. (2019) 'Barry Jenkins Pays Tribute to John Singleton: "Boyz N the Hood" Was "My Life"', *Hollywood Reporter*, online, 5 July, https://www.hol lywoodreporter.com/news/barry-jenkins-pays-tribute-john-singleton-boyz-n-ho od-1208278.

Swanson, C. (2016) '*Moonlight* Director Barry Jenkins Thought He'd Fled His Past, Then He Accidentally Made a Movie About It', *Vulture*, online, 1 December, https://www.vulture.com/2016/11/barry-jenkins-moonlight.html.

Tate, G. (2016) 'How Barry Jenkins Turned the Misery and Beauty of the Queer Black Experience Into the Year's Best Movie', *Village Voice*, online, 21 December, https://www.villagevoice.com/2016/12/21/how-barry-jenkins-tu rned-the-misery-and-beauty-of-the-queer-black-experience-into-the-years-best -movie/.

Thompson, D. (2016) 'Hollywood Has a Huge Millennial Problem', *Atlantic*, online, 8 June, https://www.theatlantic.com/business/archive/2016/06/hollywo od-has-a-huge-millennial-problem/486209/.

Thrasher, S.W. (2016) '*Moonlight* Portrays Black Gay Life in Its Joy, Sadness and Complexity', *Guardian*, online, 29 October, https://www.theguardian.com/film /2016/oct/29/moonlight-movie-barry-jenkins-black-gay.

Townsend, M. (2017) '89th Academy Awards: 'Moonlight' is First LGBTQ Film to Win Best Picture', *GLAAD News*, online, 26 February, https://www.glaad.org/ blog/89th-academy-awards-moonlight-first-lgbtq-film-win-best-picture.

Turan, K. (2016) 'Review: Barry Jenkins' Magical, Majestic 'Moonlight' Is a Stunning Portrait of Young, Black Gay Life', *Los Angeles Times*, online, 20 October, https://www.latimes.com/entertainment/movies/la-et-mn-moonlight -review-20161017-snap-story.html.

Ugwu, R. (2020) 'The Hashtag That Changed the Oscars: An Oral History', *New York Times*, online, 6 February, https://www.nytimes.com/2020/02/06/movies/ oscarssowhite-history.html.

Van Deburg, W.L. (2004) *Hoodlums: Black Villains and Social Bandits in American Life*, Chicago: University of Chicago Press.

Verstraten, P. (2019) '*Moonlight* as a "Mass Art" Film', *Senses of Cinema*, No. 92, http://sensesofcinema.com/2019/cinema-in-the-2010s/moonlight-as-a-mass-art- film/.

Wacquant L. (2010) 'Urban Desolation and Symbolic Denigration in the Hyperghetto', *Social Psychology Quarterly*, Vol. 73, No. 3, pp. 215–9.

Walcott, R. (2003) *Black Like Who?: Writing Black Canada*, Toronto: Insomniac Press.

Walcott, R. (2019) '*Moonlight*'s Necessary Company', *GLQ: A Journal of Lesbian and Gay Studies*, Vol. 25, No. 2, pp. 337–41.

Walker, B. (2017) 'The Illumination of Blackness in *Moonlight*', *A Nation of Billions*, online, 3 March, https://nationofbillions.com/the-illumination-of-b lackness-in-moonlight.

Wallace, C. (2018) 'Why "Black Panther" Is a Defining Moment for Black America', *New York Times*, online, 12 February, https://www.nytimes.com/2018/02/12/ magazine/why-black-panther-is-a-defining-moment-for-black-america.html.

Wallenberg, L. (2004) 'New Black Queer Cinema', in M. Aaron (ed) *New Queer Cinema: A Critical Reader*, Edinburgh: Edinburgh University Press, pp. 128–43.

Watkins-Hayes, C., Byrd R. and Merritt, C. (2019) 'Eclipsed: Darkness, Light, and Motherhood in the Sexualized Drug Economy of *Moonlight*', *Western Journal of Black Studies*, Vol. 42, Nos. 3–4, pp. 81–9.

Whipp, G. (2016) '"*Moonlight* Changed Me", Says Director Barry Jenkins of his Emotional Story of Acceptance', *Los Angeles Times*, online, 1 December, https://www.latimes.com/entertainment/envelope/la-en-mn-barry-jenkins-moonlight-20161121-story.html.

White, A. (2016) '*Moonlight*: A Plea for Pity for a Black, Gay Statistic', *National Review*, online, 22 October, https://www.nationalreview.com/2016/10/moonlight-barry-jenkins-intersectionality-black-gay-character/.

Wiegman, R. (1993) 'Feminism, "The Boyz", and Other Matters Regarding the Male', in S. Cohan and I. Rae Hark (eds) *Screening the Male: Exploring Masculinities in Hollywood Cinema*, London: Routledge, pp. 173–93.

Wilson, M. (2019) 'Eat Your Feelings: Food, Consumption, and Queer Subjectivity in Contemporary American Cinema', Dissertation submitted to King's College London, pp. 1–37.

Wojcik-Andrews, I. (2000) *Children's Films: History, Ideology, Pedagogy, Theory*, London: Garland Publishing.

Wyatt, J. (1993) 'Cinematic/Sexual Transgression: An Interview with Todd Haynes', *Film Quarterly*, Vol. 46, No. 3, pp. 2–8.

Yancy, G. (2016 [2008]) *Black Bodies, White Gazes: The Continuing Significance of Race in America*, 2nd edition, Lanham, MA: Rowman and Littlefield.

Yancy, G. (2017) 'Introduction: Dangerous Conversations', in G. Yancy (ed) *On Race: 34 Conversations in a Time of Crisis*, Oxford: Oxford University Press, pp. 1–14.

Yancy, G. (2019) 'Guest Editor Introduction: *Moonlight*: The Weight of "Intimacy"', *Western Journal of Black Studies*, Vol. 42, Nos. 3–4, pp. 65–9.

Zaman, F. (2016) '*Moonlight*: The 54th New York Film Festival', *Film Comment*, September-October, p. 42.

Index

Printed in the United States
by Baker & Taylor Publisher Services